# TEACHING BILINGUAL CHILDREN:
# BELIEFS AND BEHAVIORS

Suzanne Irujo

**A TeacherSource Book**

Donald Freeman
*Series Editor*

**THOMSON**

**HEINLE**

LEARNING AND INFORMATION
SERVICES
UNIVERSITY OF CUMBRIA

Australia  Canada  Mexico  Singapore  Spain  United Kingdom  United States

# Thank You

The series editor, authors and publisher would like to thank the following individuals who offered many helpful insights throughout the development of the *TeacherSource* series.

| | |
|---|---|
| Linda Lonon Blanton | University of New Orleans |
| Tommie Brasel | New Mexico School for the Deaf |
| Jill Burton | University of South Australia |
| Margaret B. Cassidy | Brattleboro Union High School, Vermont |
| Florence Decker | University of Texas at El Paso |
| Silvia G. Diaz | Dade County Public Schools, Florida |
| Margo Downey | Boston University |
| Alvino Fantini | School for International Training |
| Sandra Fradd | University of Miami |
| Jerry Gebhard | Indiana University of Pennsylvania |
| Fred Genesee | University of California at Davis |
| Stacy Gildenston | Colorado State University |
| Jeannette Gordon | Illinois Resource Center |
| Else Hamayan | Illinois Resource Center |
| Sarah Hudelson | Arizona State University |
| Joan Jamieson | Northern Arizona University |
| Elliot L. Judd | University of Illinois at Chicago |
| Donald N. Larson | Bethel College, Minnesota (Emeritus) |
| Numa Markee | University of Illinois at Urbana Champaign |
| Denise E. Murray | San Jose State University |
| Meredith Pike-Baky | University of California at Berkeley |
| Sara L. Sanders | Coastal Carolina University |
| Donna Sievers | Garden Grove Unified School District, California |
| Leo van Lier | Monterey Institute of International Studies |

The publication of *Teaching Bilingual Children: Beliefs and Behaviors* was directed by members of the Newbury House ESL/EFL Team at Heinle:

Erik Gundersen, Editorial Director
Bruno R. Paul, Marketing Director
Kristin M. Thalheimer, Production Services Coordinator
Thomas Healy, Developmental Editor
Stanley J. Galek, Vice President and Publisher/ESL

Also participating in the publication of this program were:

**Project Manager, Designer, and Compositor:** Imageset Design/Mary Reed
**Manufacturing Coordinator:** Mary Beth Hennebury
**Associate Market Development Director:** Mary Sutton
**Cover Designer:** Ha D. Nguyen

Heinle is a division of International Thomson Publishing, Inc.

Manufactured in the United States of America

ISBN 0-8384-6098-4

10  9  8  7  6  5  4  3

# TABLE OF CONTENTS

# ACKNOWLEDGMENTS

This book would not have been possible without the cooperation of "Matilde," the teacher whose voice permeates the book, whose willingness to be herself in front of an observer allowed me to record the reality of a bilingual classroom and whose beliefs and behaviors provide the practice in which to ground my theory. I'm sure there were days when she wished I wasn't there, and I know there are incidents recorded here that she would rather forget, but she was always gracious and helpful. Thanks also to the children in her classroom and to their parents for permission to observe the children and use examples of their work.

The book would also not have been possible without Donald Freeman's idea for a different kind of teacher resource book, his belief in my ability to write the book, and his friendship. Nor would it have been possible without Heinle & Heinle's support of Donald's concept for this series, and without the guidance of David Lee, Erik Gundersen, and Thomas Healy.

I am grateful to the members of the Language Teacher Educators Collaborative: Francis Bailey, Donald Freeman, Maggie Hawkins, Kathleen Graves, Diane Larsen-Freeman, Ellen Rintell, and Jerri Willet. Our discussions provided a catalyst for my thinking as I wrote and pushed me to look beyond what I thought I believed about teaching and learning.

Finally, an immense thank you to my husband, Peter Barck, for his patience in letting me bounce ideas off him, his willingness to read the manuscript and let me know when my prose was foggy, his understanding while the book was consuming all of my time, his technical expertise, and his belief in me.

# PREFACE

Driving just south of White River Junction, the snow had started falling in earnest. The light was flat, although it was mid-morning, making it almost impossible to distinguish the highway in the gray-white swirling snow. I turned on the radio, partly as a distraction and partly to help me concentrate on the road ahead; the announcer was talking about the snow. "The state highway department advises motorists to use extreme caution and to drive with their headlights on to ensure maximum visibility." He went on, his tone shifting slightly, "Ray Burke, the state highway supervisor, just called to say that one of the plows almost hit a car just south of Exit 6 because the person driving hadn't turned on his lights. He really wants people to put their headlights on because it is very tough to see in this stuff." I checked, almost reflexively, to be sure that my headlights were on, as I drove into the churning snow.

How can information serve those who hear or read it in making sense of their own worlds? How can it enable them to reason about what they do and to take appropriate actions based on that reasoning? My experience with the radio in the snowstorm illustrates two different ways of providing the same message: the need to use your headlights when you drive in heavy snow. The first offers dispassionate information; the second tells the same content in a personal, compelling story. The first disguises its point of view; the second explicitly grounds the general information in a particular time and place. Each means of giving information has its role, but I believe the second is ultimately more useful in helping people make sense of what they are doing. When I heard Ray Burke's story about the plow, I made sure my headlights were on.

In what is written about teaching, it is rare to find accounts in which the author's experience and point of view are central. A point of view is not simply an opinion; neither is it a whimsical or impressionistic claim. Rather, a point of view lays out what the author thinks and why. To borrow the phrase from writing teacher Natalie Goldberg, "it sets down the bones." The problem is that much of what is available in professional development in language-teacher education concentrates on telling rather than on point of view. The telling is prescriptive, like the radio announcer's first statement. It emphasizes what is important to know and do, what is current in theory and research, and therefore what you—as a practicing teacher—should do. But this telling disguises the teller; it hides the point of view that can enable you to make sense of what is told.

The **TeacherSource** series offers you a point of view on second/foreign language teaching. Each author in this series has had to lay out what she or he believes is central to the topic, and how she or he has come to this understanding. So as a reader, you will find this book has a personality; it is not anonymous. It comes as a story, not as a directive, and it is meant to create a relationship with you rather than assume your attention. As a practitioner, its point of view can help you in your own work by providing a sounding board for your ideas and a metric for your own thinking. It can suggest courses of action and explain why these make sense to the author. And you can take from it what you will, and do with it what you can. This book will not tell you what to think; it is meant to help you make sense of what you do.

The point of view in **TeacherSource** is woven out of three strands: **Teachers' Voices, Frameworks, and Investigations.** Each author draws together these strands uniquely, as suits his or her topic and more crucially his or her point of view. All materials in TeacherSource have these three strands. The **Teachers' Voices** are practicing language teachers from various settings who tell about their experience of the topic. The **Frameworks** lay out what the author believes is important to know about his or her topic and its key concepts and issues. These fundamentals define the area of language teaching and learning about which she or he is writing. The **Investigations** are meant to engage you, the reader, in relating the topic to your own teaching, students, and classroom. They are activities which you can do, alone or with colleagues, to reflect on teaching and learning and/or try out ideas in practice.

Each strand offers a point of view on the book's topic. The **Teachers' Voices** relate the points of view of various practitioners; the **Frameworks** establish the point of view of the professional community; and the **Investigations** invite you to develop your own point of view, through experience with reference to your setting. Together these strands should serve in making sense of the topic.

In Suzanne Irujo's book, we meet a second-grade teacher, Matilde, and her students. Through a small-scale ethnography, Irujo has us spend time in this classroom over the course of a year, examining the learning and teaching that go on there. Matilde is not intended to be a model of how to teach; as Irujo says, hers "is simply the reality of one classroom." With this grounding in actual teaching, Irujo introduces nine themes as frameworks for understanding bilingual education. Hers is a commited examination of what can make education in two languages work for children. As someone who has spent her career in these settings, Irujo brings a depth and richness to thinking about educating children bilingually that goes well beyond the polemics which often surround public debates on the topic. Her book engages the reader in examining both the theories and practices which shape bilingual education to figure out what makes sense to do and why.

This book, like all elements of the **TeacherSource** series, is intended to serve you in understanding your work as a language teacher. It may lead you to thinking about what you do in different ways and/or to taking specific actions in your teaching. Or it may do neither. But we intend, through the variety of points of view presented in this fashion, to offer you access to choices in teaching that you may not have thought of before and thus to help your teaching make more sense.

*—Donald Freeman, Series Editor*

# BEGINNING: ABOUT THE BOOK

Schoolrooms without children in them seem unnaturally empty. In Room 7 of the Washington School, the bulletin boards display their contents to the empty air. There is nobody to see the map display showing where the children are from, no students to proudly point out the bulletin board with their perfect papers displaying work that is "Super, Great, Tops, Neat, Wow." The alphabet picture cards proclaim only to themselves that *avion* begins with *a* and *bicicleta* begins with *b*. The computers sit with dark faces, waiting to come to life so they can help with writing and mathematics. The bins of books that occupy every flat surface in the room becken to absent children to rummage through their contents. The songs and poems that hang from chartholders at various places around the room and the **big books** sitting on easels all wait patiently for somebody to read them.

Shortly after 8:30 the teacher comes in, arms full of boxes of materials. Matilde has been teaching in this same room for enough years now that it should be well stocked with arts and crafts materials, math manipulatives, and all kinds of things to read and to write on, but still she brings more in each day.

Matilde got into teaching by accident. She had a college degree and was bilingual, and the school system needed bilingual teachers. After a few years' teaching bilingual special education, she decided that it wasn't what she really wanted to do. *"I was determined to leave the system. I received a couple of job offers, and I said I wouldn't take them. I just said no, I'm not looking for a job, and I refused to accept. Towards August, one of my friends who was still working in the system kept trying to convince me, so I really thought hard about it. It was almost the day school opened that I decided to accept this position. It's been going well, and I've been here ever since. I like this school building better than any other building I've worked in. I like being a teacher here because I'm given a chance to be creative, do different types of activities with the children. The principal has been very supportive, which is really important, and I've also had a chance to take lots of courses, to enhance what I do with the children."*

The school that Matilde likes so much is a big old two-story rectangular brick building, with eight classrooms on each floor. The rooms are large, with high

Words and phrases in **bold print** are defined in the glossary.

ceilings and tall windows that have to be opened from the top with long window poles. Each classroom has a coatroom attached to it that's the size of some classrooms in newer schools. In spite of its age, the building is well cared for, freshly painted, neat, and clean, with colorful displays of student work on every available wall space. The school houses kindergarten through grade four classes, half of them Spanish bilingual and half English monolingual.

Matilde puts away the materials she has brought in. She is professionally dressed in coordinated shades of beige and brown, with large gold earrings and pins that balance her large frame. Her short curly brown hair is arranged neatly around a face that always seems to be smiling. Even when her mouth is not actually turned up at the corners, the sparkle in her large brown eyes says, "I'm glad you're here."

Matilde's closet is a treasure chest of presents for birthdays or perfect attendance, paper plates and cups for parties, dehydrated soups for emergency lunches, all kinds of materials for art projects. While she is putting things away, she hears a cheery "Good morning!" as the first of her students enters the room. Yoni has only been here for a few weeks, but he has already learned one of the implicit codes of the classroom: morning greetings are in English.

Yoni is one of those children who manages to look dirty and sloppy even when he is clean and neat. His head exhibits the season's preferred haircut among young boys: very short on the back and sides, longer on top, with a corkscrew curl left hanging down the back of his neck. It looks like somebody put a bowl over his head and shaved everything that wasn't covered by the bowl, forgetting one little strand in the back.

As Yoni goes to the coatroom other children come in, each in turn saying "Good morning." Several of the other boys have the same haircut as Yoni. The children hang up their coats and go to their desks to put their backpacks over the backs of their chairs. Backpacks seem to be part of the unwritten uniform of second graders.

A few of the children cluster around the teacher's desk, talking about what they did yesterday, about their homework, about what happened on the bus this morning. Matilde asks Nina about the book in her hand, "Is this a good book?" Nina replies, *"Es de las mariposas,"* ("It's about butterflies,") and the bilingual conversation continues, Matilde commenting in English and Nina replying in Spanish. When Ángela comes in, Matilde greets her with,

| | |
|---|---|
| *"Hola, ¿cómo estás?* | ("Hi, how are you? What |
| *¿Qué pasó el viernes,* | happened on Friday, that you |
| *que tú no veniste? No me* | didn't come? You're not going |
| *vas a molestar hoy, ¿verdad?* | to bother me today, right?) |

"OK, you guys are my witness, she's not going to bother me today," she announces to the others. Ángela is a beautiful child with a round brown face and long, straight black hair, always worn falling loosely down her back. She is newly arrived from Guatemala, with no previous schooling. Her curiosity, her desire to know everything that's going on, her gossipy nature, and her resemblance to a wise old Mayan woman have combined to earn her the nickname *La viejita* (Little Old Lady), affectionately used by everyone in the class.

Other children go directly to their desks and take out their journals. This classroom code is explicit. When you come into school in the morning, the first thing you do is get out your journal, write a paragraph, and draw a picture about what you wrote. Talking to the teacher when you first come in may postpone the task briefly. Working on something else instead, such as math books or writing folders, may delay the task a little longer. But at some point in the morning, Matilde is going to say in a stern voice,

"*¿Qué tienen que hacer cuando llegan por la mañana?*" ("What do you have to do when you get here in the morning?")

Matilde is one of those teachers with a presence, and she doesn't have to speak loudly to sound stern. Her soft voice carries dual messages whenever she speaks. The words convey what she is talking about, but the modulations show what she is feeling toward the person to whom she is talking. Most of the time the modulations say things like, "I care about you," "I enjoy being your teacher," or "I'm very pleased with your work." Sometimes they say things like, "I know you can do better than this," or "I don't like the way you're behaving." Occasionally they say, "I'm angry with you." So far this morning the modulations have been concerned and caring, as Matilde talks about having seen two of the children at the mall the previous day. The words say,

"*Ayer yo me fui al* mall *porque iba a llevar a la nena para tomar unas fotos, pero llegué tarde, y después empecé a comprar, dando vueltas con Sarina, comprando cosas, jugo y soda y cosas que tenía que comprar. Entonces alguien decía 'Matilde,' y fue Teresa. Estuve charlando con ella, después vino su mamá con su hermanita, y me despedí de ellos. Nos metimos allí a comer en* Little Caesar's, *y me encontré con esta chiquita, con Inés, que entró a comprar pizza.*" ("Yesterday I went to the mall because I was going to take my little girl to have some pictures taken, but I got there late, and then I began to buy stuff, just going around with Sarina, buying things, juice and soda and things that I had to buy. Then somebody said 'Matilde,' and it was Teresa. I was chatting with her, and then her mother came with her little sister, and then I said goodbye to them. We went into Little Caesar's to eat, and I ran into this little girl, Inés, who came in to buy pizza.")

The modulations say, "I'm glad that I saw you at the mall." The talk continues about what the children did the previous day, with the modulations in Matilde's comments saying, "I'm really interested in everything you do outside of school."

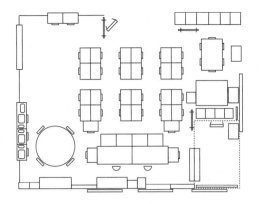

Matilde is sitting in a student-sized chair in front of the blackboard while she talks with the children. Now she stands up, turns to the blackboard, draws lines on it with a multichalk holder, and turns back to the children. "OK, what are we going to write? *Mariana, ¿qué hiciste?* (Mariana, what did you do?) You went to the park? Evita? You went where? You went to Toys 'R' Us? You went shopping? You had a birthday party at your house? How old are you now? 20? Lucy, you went to Chuck E. Cheese's? I haven't been there yet. Maybe I'll take Sarina."

From the contributions of the children, Matilde helps the class create a short narrative, which she writes on the board as the children dictate. "OK, so you guys went to Chuck E. Cheese's, you went to the park, you went to the East River, some kids went to the mall. So can we write about what we did on the weekend?"

Mariana begins, *"Ayer yo fui a…"* ("Yesterday I went to…")

"No, we're doing it in English."

"Yesterday I…"

"Can we talk about how nice it was yesterday?" Matilde writes on the board, reading slowly and clearly as she writes, "Yesterday was a very hot and beautiful day."

"OK, what happened?" she says, and continues writing: "We had fun, we went to the park, the mall and Chucky E. Cheese's [sic]."

Without having been asked, Liana is passing out lined paper. The children silently begin copying the story from the board. When they finish they show their papers to Matilde, who may remind them to be sure to get the capital letters and punctuation right. She then puts the neatest papers up on the bulletin board, where good work is displayed.

Later in the morning, most of the children are working quietly at their seats, completing pages in their math books, writing in their journals or their writing folders, or drawing pictures to illustrate what they have written. There is a low buzz, but it is purposeful talk—talk that is necessary to accomplish the task at hand, and always done in a soft voice so as not to disturb others in their work. There is a calmness in the air, a feeling that everybody knows what to do and is busy doing it.

The variety of activities is astonishing. It almost seems that no two children are doing the same thing. Nina is writing in her journal. She composes a few sentences about what she did the previous evening and draws a picture to accompany what she wrote. Marisol is at the computer using a children's word processing program called the Bank Street Writer to do her journal entry. When she finishes, she waits for her composition to print out and takes the paper back to her seat to do her illustration. Another child slips into place at the computer almost immediately. There is no sign-up sheet and no discussion—one child finishes and another begins.

Matilde is sitting at the listening center table with Camilo. They each have a copy of an identical book in their hands, and Matilde is listening to Camilo as he reads aloud. Across the room, Yoni and Liana are sitting at their desks, also holding identical books. Yoni is reading from a small copy of a big book that has been read to the class many times. As he reads aloud, Liana helps him whenever he has trouble with a word.

Several children are working in math books, doing different problems on different pages of different books. Omar gets up and takes his math book to Matilde. They confer briefly about something in the book, and he goes back to his seat.

The rest of the children are in their seats, reading or writing, doing word search puzzles or worksheets. Occasionally one gets up to get a book or put one back. The classroom aide is correcting homework. She calls Rosita to her desk and explains something that was incorrect. Rosita takes the paper back to her seat and corrects the work.

The overall impression is one of purpose. The children all seem to know what they have to do and they do it. Only occasionally does Matilde have to remind Fernando and Teresa that they need to finish something instead of talking so much.

---

This is a book about children. It is about how children learn, and about what teachers can do to help children learn better. In many ways it is not really a book about **bilingual education**. It is about good education that happens to focus on bilingual children. Bilingual children need advocates because the political issues surrounding bilingual education tend to overshadow the educational issues, and the children get lost in the process. This book has therefore been written for teachers, administrators, and others who are concerned with the education of bilingual children.

Part of this book is based on the description of an actual bilingual classroom. Since the native language of the children in that classroom is Spanish, a lot of Spanish is used in the book. However, the same kinds of things occur with children from other language backgrounds, and most of the issues discussed are applicable to all bilingual children, regardless of whether they are in bilingual classrooms.

Except for the chapter on language use, the rest of the book is applicable to any children, bilingual or not. There is nothing different about how bilingual children learn, except that they do it in two languages. It must be remembered that bilingual programs are not meant to be language programs; they are educational programs whose main purpose is to ensure the cognitive development of the students. Collier (1995a, 1995b) found that one of the key factors promoting academic success is cognitively complex instruction through the first language for as long as possible. Use of the native language facilitates cognitive development, so it should be used. In discussing language use in bilingual classrooms, I do not further address the question of whether the native language should be used. My premise is that anything that can help a child learn should be used, and the use of the native language can help children learn. Any further debate becomes political.

I learned a lot of what I know about elementary education on the job. With a degree in secondary education and Spanish, and the desire to become a high school Spanish teacher, I began my teaching career in a third- and fourth-grade bilingual classroom. I had no idea how to teach reading, or math, or whatever else third- and fourth-grade students are supposed to learn. I couldn't even imagine what elementary school teachers did with the same children all day long. The few textbooks that I found in my classroom were useless as instructional materials. What was I to do with reading books that asked children to read nonsense such as "See Spot run," or "A pig can jig"? How was I to teach multiplication when I had no math books other than a series of entirely non-verbal programmed texts in which multiplication did not appear until Book 21 and most of the students had given up in boredom sometime after Book 10?

I relied mostly on intuition those first years, reading to the children a lot and exploring language through games and songs and real things. We went on walks, bringing back tadpoles and caterpillars and watching them turn into frogs and butterflies. We made maps of the school, the neighborhood, the city. We published a class newspaper. What I was doing made sense to me, and the children were excited about learning. Although their formal learning was not measured against any objective criteria, they made a lot of progress, and I believed in their potential.

I decided that if I was going to be a bilingual teacher I should know something about what I was doing, so I enrolled in a master's program in bilingual education. I learned a lot about psycholinguistics, sociolinguistics, and contrastive analysis, but very little about elementary education. So I began to talk with other teachers in the school, observing what they did in their classrooms. I discovered that I wasn't doing it "right." I was supposed to have reading groups, seatwork, workbooks, textbooks, worksheets, tests... I decided that these other teachers must know much more about elementary education than I did, since they had degrees in it and a lot of experience. So I organized reading groups, spent hours and hours planning seatwork, brought the **basal readers** and the workbooks out of the closet, ran off multiple copies of multiple worksheets, gave my students tests...

Some time after that I began having recurring nightmares that I was standing in front of my class first thing in the morning, and I hadn't prepared enough seatwork to get me through the day. And sometime after *that*, I realized that teaching wasn't as much fun as it had been at first. Although the children were good about doing whatever work I asked of them, they were no longer excited about learning. I began to think of them as "dumb" because they were having such a hard time doing the exercises in the texts and the workbooks. I didn't question what I was doing, however, because I believed that I was now doing it "right."

Some time after that, I found myself yelling at the children and criticizing them to other teachers. It was time for a change. Teaching wasn't fun any more, and I certainly didn't want to be the kind of teacher who yelled. I left the classroom to get a doctoral degree. I now work as a teacher educator with elementary and secondary ESL and bilingual teachers. I have learned a lot about elementary education, as well as about how language and literacy are learned. I now believe that I was doing it "right" when I first started to teach. I was doing things that made sense, and I believe that "making sense" is the essence of learning. Whether it's learning how to fix a car, speak another language, program a computer, or understand philosophy, when we want to learn something, we work at the task in various ways until it makes sense to us. Why, then, do we ask children in elementary schools to do so many senseless tasks?

When I began teaching elementary school I used a holistic approach simply because it made sense to me. Years later I found that what I had been doing was similar to what people are now calling **whole language**. Similarly, I became convinced that the learning children do is a result of their own efforts, and that a teacher only facilitates that process. Recently I found out that these beliefs are part of a theory of learning called **constructivism**.

This book reflects the principles of both whole language and constructivism, although I prefer not to use these labels because my beliefs were formed before I knew the labels. I would prefer to simply call it "making sense." That idea is not original to me. I owe a lot to Carole Edelsky (1991) and Frank Smith (1975, 1986) for my understanding of this deceptively simple view of what teaching and learning are about. My debt to them, and to others who have influenced my thinking with their passionate belief in education as "making sense," is explained and acknowledged throughout this book.

The principles of constructivism and whole language apply to adults' learning as well as to children's. Because I believe that adults learn in the same ways children do, I have tried to write a book that will help teachers and other readers make sense of their own experiences. If we believe, as Poplin states, that "the natural sequence in which [learners]... construct new meanings is from whole to part to whole" (1993, p. 60), then teachers need a sense of how the whole of teaching functions in order to be able to fit individual teaching skills together and make sense of them. If we believe that "the learner transforms new experiences through what he/she currently knows and believes" (ibid.), then it is important for teachers to become aware of what they know and believe. If we believe that "learning is self-regulated and self-preserving (not teacher or curriculum regulated)" (ibid., p. 61), then prospective or practicing teachers will learn best whatever they choose to learn and whatever they are interested in. If we believe that "meanings are constructed not only individually but socially" (ibid.), then teachers must be given opportunities to work together.

This book attempts to put these principles into practice in various ways. The whole of one particular teaching situation is presented in the Teachers' Voices strand. This part of the book provides a comprehensive view of one elementary bilingual classroom through the eyes of an observer in that classroom. The Teachers' Voices strand is not meant to be a model of what should or should not occur in a bilingual classroom. No attempt is made to judge whether the events in this classroom are good, mediocre, or bad. Everything is simply presented the way it happened, a verbal snapshot of a real classroom at the present time.

Examples of how my knowledge and beliefs have been shaped by my experiences are presented in the Frameworks strand. This part of the book is a compilation of my own experiences and those of others who have influenced me: my teaching experience, my work with pre- and in-service bilingual teachers, and key works that have had a profound influence on me. This strand attempts to convey to the reader what I believe and why. I hope it will provide new experiences for the reader and new ways of looking at familiar experiences.

The organization of topics within the Frameworks strand is one of ever-widening concentric circles, beginning with the child and progressing outward through classroom and school to community. The first theme looks at children and at my beliefs about how children learn and why many children have trouble learning in some school situations. The second and third themes look at the kinds of activities that facilitate children's learning, activities that are authentic and that give children chances to learn by doing. The fourth and fifth themes look at lessons through the methods teachers use and the planning that goes into creating lessons. The sixth and seventh themes look at two important aspects of classrooms: the use of technology in classrooms, and the use of two languages in bilingual classrooms. The eighth theme looks at the school-wide issue of how students should be assessed, and the ninth theme looks at how the community affects the classroom through culture.

Opportunities for you, the reader, to transform the teacher's experiences, my experiences, and your own experiences are presented in the Investigations strand. In that part of the book you will interpret these new experiences through what you already know. It will provide a means to include your voice in the book, allowing you to contribute your own experiences, beliefs, and theories to the discussion. Activities that are part of the Investigations strand are found throughout the book.

Readers of this book will necessarily self-regulate their learning by using it in whatever way works best for them. I have tried to structure the book so it will be flexible enough to be used in many different ways. I hope readers will capitalize on the social nature of learning by sharing activities and discussions with colleagues.

The book can be read in many different ways. You don't have to begin on page 1 and read in a linear fashion. The margin notes will help you connect the same theme across the three strands of the book. Thus if you are reading about a particular theme in the Teachers' Voices strand, a Frameworks margin note will guide you to the appropriate pages for the theoretical background about that theme. You may want to go to those pages and read the discussion right then, or you may want to read all of the Teachers' Voices strand before you begin the Frameworks.

Reading the entire Teachers' Voices strand first will give you a complete picture of the reality of this particular classroom. If you do this, you will probably want to refer back to particular sections of "The Teacher" when you read the Frameworks. Use the Teachers' Voices margin notes to help you do that.

Investigation activities are found throughout the book, some as part of the text, some in margin notes, and some in a separate section at the end of the book. All of the Investigations are identified by margin notes, and at the beginning of the book there is a description of the kinds of activities included in the Investigations strand. Don't think that you have to do all of the Investigations. Whether they are assigned by instructors using the book as a text or chosen by teachers reading the book on their own, only the activities that seem most useful and appropriate should be done.

Whether you start at the beginning and read every page to the end or continually jump around following the margin notes wherever they send you, whether you choose the themes that interest you most and read them first or just dip into the book wherever it happens to open, I hope your enjoyment and benefit from reading it are as great as mine were in writing it.

This is a Frameworks margin note.

This is a Teachers' Voices margin note.

This is an Investigations margin note.

Investigations

# INVESTIGATIONS

*All Investigations activities are identified by the Investigations icon in the margin. Margin Notes, Observations, Journals, and Reflections are included in the Teachers' Voices and Frameworks strands. Classroom Research, Case Studies, and other projects are described in the separate Investigations section at the end of the book.*

**Margin Notes:** These are short prompts in the margins suggesting topics for discussion with colleagues or for note-taking while reading. Discussion and note-taking may be interchanged, or the prompts can be the basis for an ongoing reflective journal.

**Observations:** These are suggestions for observing in your own or someone else's classroom in order to connect what you read in the Teachers' Voices strand with similar or different practices in other situations.

**Journal:** This is an opportunity for you to write down what you believe about a particular aspect of teaching before reading about it in the Frameworks strand. Of course, journal entries need not be limited to the Investigations activities that call for them; I would encourage you to keep an ongoing journal of your thoughts while you are teaching, observing, and reading.

**Reflection:** This is a prompt designed to help you relate what you read in a Frameworks theme to what was depicted in Matilde's classroom. The Reflection prompts come at the end of each theme in the Frameworks strand.

**Classroom Research:** This is an activity that incorporates reflection, observation (either in your own classroom or in somebody else's), planning for change, implementing it if you are doing the research in your own classroom, and observing what happens when you implement change. Although there is one project for each theme, you should not try to do all of them.

**Case Study:** This is a description of a situation in which a teacher or student finds him- or herself, with a series of questions designed to help readers of the case study decide what could be done in that situation. After a case study is prepared, it should be discussed with a group of colleagues.

**Other:** There are two opportunities for discourse analysis, which give the reader a chance to analyze longer sections of discourse from Matilde's classroom in order to discover underlying belief patterns. There are also several miscellaneous activities.

More information about classroom research can be found in *Doing Teacher Research: From Inquiry to Understanding* in the *TeacherSource* series.

# THE
# TEACHER

There are 25 children in Matilde's second-grade classroom. All of them speak Spanish as their native language. Some also spoke English when they began school; some did not. Some have learned a lot of English since they began school; some have not. Some have been in this school since kindergarten; others arrived this year. Some of the new arrivals have been in school before; some have not. Some are very intelligent; some, less so. Some work hard, others do not.

The children are from Puerto Rico, the Dominican Republic, Colombia, Venezuela, Honduras, El Salvador, Guatemala, and the United States. Some are United States citizens; some are immigrants. Some of the immigrants are legal; some are not. All of them are "minority" students. All come from low-income families and receive free breakfast and lunch at school. Some of their parents are more able than others to help their children with schoolwork, but all care about their children's success in school.

Matilde believes that this group's overall achievement level is low. She repeats several times over the course of the months of observation that she is not happy with their level for the time of year. At the end of the year, however, she defends them from complaints about their low level from the third-grade teacher. *"I explained to her about the different levels that the children are on, and she was like, 'Oh, my, they seem to be very low.' And I said, 'Well, remember, I'm telling you about children that came here in April last year, that didn't have any prior schooling, so where they are now, it's great, you know, considering.' And she said, 'And you're going to pass them?' and I said, 'Yes, because I feel as though they can do well, but you're going to have to give them the support that they need, also some individualized work, and maybe some extra work to take home.' So she said, 'Well, it seems that this was a group that can function.' I said, 'Yeah, they can function, they can do quite well.'"*

Most of the children are 7 or 8 years old, with two 9-year-olds. Their reading levels range from Yoni, who is a nonreader in both languages, to Lucy and Diara, who can read at or above grade level, fluently and with good compre-

**Frameworks**

Bilingual
Children
Learn,
pp. 63-66.

**Investigations**

Discuss with a colleague whether you think Matilde's comment is a reflection of low teacher expectations or an objective statement of reality. Remember that the description of Matilde and her classroom is not meant to reflect either good or bad practice, or even "typical" conditions. It is simply the reality of one classroom.

hension, in both Spanish and English. In mathematics they range from Ángela, who has difficulty remembering what number comes before or after another, to Nicolás and Omar, who have figured out multiplication by themselves. Matilde deals with this diversity in many ways. She organizes the students into reading groups, even though the **whole language** philosophy of the school discourages that, because she feels she can meet the children's needs better that way. She uses whatever help she can to provide extra individualization: parents, volunteers, student teachers, observers... She often asks one student to help another. Her classroom is set up with centers where the children can work independently when they have finished their assignments. Few of them do so, however. Matilde calls her students "resistant." *"They still tend to come up and ask 'Can I do this?' when the rule is if you've finished doing what you had assigned for you to do, you have the privilege to go to the computers, go to the shared reading area, go to the listening center, or even do a little art work."*

Some of the children spend their free time reading or doing extra worksheets that are available in a box in front of Matilde's desk. Others spend a lot of time doing nothing. Jorge is one of the children who would rather sit and daydream than read or write, although he does enjoy doing mathematics. He is a small, slim boy with dark brown hair, brown eyes, and a light complexion. When engaged in conversation, he speaks very well in Spanish, politely using the formal forms of address and asking questions that show his curiosity about many things. He has a tendency to clown around, making funny faces and giggling. At times, however, he is lethargic, refusing to talk about anything, sitting with his head down on his desk and staring out the window. Jorge went to first grade in Colombia, and he says he would rather live there than here. He had friends there and others to talk to and play with. Here he lives alone with his mother, who is afraid to let him go outside and play. He spends most of his time at home watching television. He seems to understand most of what goes on in English, but almost never produces any English himself.

One day in April, Jorge starts the day coloring a picture with magic markers. He puts them away when Nicolás begins reviewing the spelling words for the week and joins with the rest of the class in reading the words from flash cards:

| | |
|---|---|
| *animales, diario, gestos,* | (animals, diary, gestures, |
| *aplaudimos, cruzar, cueva,* | we applaud, to cross, cave, |
| *guitarra, meterse, armadillo,* | guitar, to go in, armadillo, |
| *violín* | violin) |

When the children begin suggesting sentences for each spelling word, Jorge makes comments about them under his breath, giggling and making faces at each sentence contributed. As the class begins clapping out the syllables in each word, he claps on the sides of his head between words, repeats each word after everybody else in the class has said it, and states the wrong number of syllables for each word, even though he has clapped them correctly.

Next is a mathematics lesson taught by a student teacher. Jorge begins to do the paper as soon as it is passed out, without waiting for explanations. When he is asked to put his pencil down and pay attention he does so, but accompanies the student teacher's explanations with exaggerated facial expressions, gestures, and a lot of pencil fiddling and eye rubbing. When the explanation is finished, Jorge completes the paper quickly and hands it to the student teacher. He then sits down and takes his journal out of his desk, but puts it right back and instead takes out a stack of little pieces of paper, each with part of a picture of a tulip on it. He spends the next half hour trying to put these puzzle pieces together.

Listening to the student teacher read a story Jorge is attentive, if a bit fidgety. Then the student teacher introduces an autobiographical writing project by talking about where the children were born, how many brothers and sisters they have, and who they live with. Giving the students papers with their names and birthdates on them, she asks them to write about themselves. It takes Jorge ten minutes to write *Yo naci en un ospital.* (I was born in a ospital.) (Spelling errors that occur in student writing are maintained in the transcriptions and translations in order to give a feeling for the original writing.)

When recess is announced, Jorge is the first to get up and go to the coatroom, but the last to come out and get in line. After recess he returns to his autobiography. Twenty minutes after they return from recess, the children line up for lunch. On his autobiography, Jorge has erased the period at the end of the sentence he had written previously and added *de Boston masachuces.*

After lunch there is a science lesson taught in English by the science specialist. During the explanation part of the lesson, Jorge becomes engrossed in stuffing his jacket into itself so it forms a little sack with a drawstring, in which he ties a knot so he can hang it from his chair. When it's time to do the activity, however, he seems to know exactly what to do. He carefully traces his hand, measures the length of the fingers, and makes a graph of the measurements. This is all very neatly done, with much erasing and redoing.

After the science teacher leaves, Matilde asks Liana to pass out yellow paper and explains that she is going to give a sentence dictation to check for *"mayúsculas, acentos, la puntuación, todo."* ("capital letters, accents, punctuation, everything.") Jorge stops stuffing and unstuffing his jacket from itself, stops all the mugging he's been doing all day with the student teacher and the science teacher, and becomes totally serious. He covers his paper with his right arm, writing what the teacher dictates with his left hand.

After the dictation, Matilde asks the children to practice a dance that they are going to do on their "graduation" day. Jorge says, "I don't like it" (one of the few things he has ever said in English) and makes a face, but participates in the practice. The last few minutes of the day are spent singing two spring songs, *De colores* and *Adiós, nieve,* as the children get their coats, organize their backpacks, and get ready to go home.

Marisol is not the reluctant reader Jorge is. She reads very well in Spanish and is beginning to read in English, although she often pronounces English words as if they were Spanish. She prefers to speak English, but unconsciously mixes the two languages when it's easier to say something in one language than in the other.

Marisol is from Venezuela, and has been in this school since kindergarten. Her mother comes to the school often to talk with Matilde about Marisol's progress or to bring something that Marisol has forgotten. She is a tall woman who pays a lot of attention to how she looks, and this same attention is evident in Marisol's color-coordinated outfits and the many different ways in which her curly black hair is arranged. A tall girl with an air of superiority, Marisol's lack of attention and busybody manner lead Matilde to become impatient with her at times.

Marisol begins the day talking with the observer and watching the process of note-taking on the laptop computer. When she is sent back to her desk to do some work, Marisol gets out her math book and does a little math, but soon gets up and goes to the teacher's desk. Ignored as Matilde counts the bottles that the children have brought in for a school fundraising drive, Marisol goes back to her desk. A few minutes later, Matilde asks her to take the bottles downstairs. When she returns, she gets out her journal, stamps the date in it, and begins writing. This is interrupted by Matilde spraying shaving cream on everybody's desks; it is housekeeping day. The children rub shaving cream all over their desks and then sponge it off. Marisol does her own desk and also the empty one next to her. She then takes everything out of her desk, putting it back in two neat piles, carefully following Matilde's instructions for what goes on the left and the right.

With her desk clean and neat, Marisol goes to the box where Matilde leaves extra worksheets for the children to do in their spare time. She doesn't take one, but instead moves to the bin that holds books with Native American themes. She thumbs through a couple of the books, and then returns to her seat with a book called *Children of the Earth and Sky*. She reads a little on the first page and then flips through the rest of the book without reading. She closes the book, looks at the pictures on the front and back covers, and gets up and puts it back.

The next five minutes are spent discussing pencils with Inés and Nina, and then Marisol settles down to finish writing in her journal and to draw the picture that accompanies each journal entry. This is what she writes (when the children began writing journals in first grade the teacher drew arrows down the page to show them where to write; some of them have retained this custom):

| | |
|---|---|
| → Ayer yo fui a la casa de mi | → *Yesterday I went to the house of my* |
| → prima Maria Alejandra. Nostros | → *cousin Maria Alexandra. We* |
| → y simos una fiesta. ¡Nose de que | → *sell abrated a party. I don't know what* |
| → era pero fui! Mi tio fue con migo. | → *it was for but I went; My uncle went a long with me.* |
| → yo comi muchos pepitos y me | → *I ate a lot of pickles and my* |
| → duelio mucho el estomago. | → *stomach hurted a lot.* |
| → yo fui solo con mitio y mi prima. | → *I went alone with myuncle and my cousin.* |
| → Mi tio jugo cartas. Mi prima | → *My uncle played cards. My cousin* |

→ y yo jugamos sega. A mi me gusto    → and I played Sega. I liked
→ el juego. y mi tio gano en el juego.    → the game. And my uncle won in
                                                         the game.

Marisol then puts her journal away in her desk, gets up, and again goes to see what papers there are in the extra paper box. Again she seems to not like the selection, so she returns to her desk and looks inside. Then she goes to a spot behind Matilde's desk and comes back with a "Stationery" paper that has pictures of bees and bee hives on it. She has taken a ruler out of her desk and begun to draw lines on the paper when Matilde asks the children to put everything away.

The next hour is spent on a lesson about rhyming words. Matilde reads a **big book** to them, *Rosa y Gastón*, pointing out the rhyming words and encouraging the children to join in the reading. Marisol comments that this is her favorite book. They read another rhyming big book together, *Pan, pan, gran pan*. Then Matilde helps them transfer what they know in Spanish to English, explaining how words also rhyme in English. She reads two-line rhymes from an old-fashioned school book, encouraging the children to guess what the last word of the second line is. When Marisol suggests "ground" to finish the line "touch the…," Matilde explains that it has to rhyme with "sky." "Does 'ground' rhyme with 'sky'? You have to listen." Matilde then passes out rhyming worksheets in Spanish for the children to do. She goes through one of the worksheets in great detail, showing the children how they have to name all the pictures before they can determine which rhyme, and then asks them to do the second worksheet alone. Marisol finishes hers quickly, but does not follow directions when she staples both papers together to hand in, instead of handing in only one. When Cristóbal returns from his special education class in the middle of the lesson, Matilde asks Marisol to help him with the worksheet. Marisol is busy showing Rosita the sticker she got for doing the rhyming worksheet correctly, so the observer goes to help Cristóbal with the rhyming words. Marisol immediately interjects, "Matilde told me to help him."

Matilde then reminds the children about how they always have to do their best work because they never know when it's going to be displayed on the bulletin board. From a bulletin board that the student teacher made, she removes some construction paper cutouts on which the children had written about themselves and tells them that they're going to have to do them over.

Next is a review of spelling words. One of the sentences that Marisol suggests is a bit more imaginative than most of the other children's, although it may or may not be true: *En mi casa hay mucho humo.* (In my house there's a lot of smoke.)

After lunch the science lesson consists of a review of what the children had learned previously about butterflies and moths. They then make colorful butterflies out of paper napkins and food coloring. Marisol, Nina, and Inés help Cristóbal with his when he seems to be having trouble putting it together.

After the science lesson the children finish reviewing the spelling words and Matilde explains to them about a reading comprehension sheet that they have to do for homework. The title of the story on the worksheet is *¿Hay perro que no ladra?* (Is There a Dog that Doesn't Bark?). When Marisol asks what *ladra* means, Matilde says, *"Viejita, ¿qué hacen los perros?"* (*"Viejita*, what do dogs do?") Ángela answers, *"Guau, guau."* "OK," says Matilde, *"ladrar es el ruido que hacen los perros.* (barking is the noise that dogs make.) Marisol, do you understand the word now?"

Matilde then calls each child to her desk individually to work on the corrections on the papers she has removed from the bulletin board. While waiting, Marisol sits at her desk, not doing anything, until Matilde tells those who are waiting to take out their math books. Marisol is working in her math book when Matilde calls her. "This right here, missy, I'm very disappointed in you,

*tienes que poner más atención a lo que haces, muchísimo más. Eso parece 'haclo.' ¿Yo haclo mucho? ¿O yo hablo mucho? Siempre yo digo a Uds., quiero ver las letras bien formadas. Es muy importante."*

(you have to pay more attention to what you're doing, a lot more. That looks like 'I tcilk a lot.' I tcilk a lot? Or I talk a lot? I always tell you guys, I want to see well-formed letters. It's very important.")

Marisol spends the last few minutes before dismissal correcting the paper so Matilde can put it back on the bulletin board.

Inés is petite, always clean and well-dressed, always smiling. She speaks both English and Spanish well, although she prefers to use Spanish. She reads fairly well in Spanish, although her reading aloud shows word-for-word reading strategies and some stumbling over words. Inés seems very bright, but Matilde claims that she is lazy, and her father, who is from El Salvador, visits the school often to confer with Matilde on how they can help her do better in school. She looks charming today, her round face framed by a long dark braid down the side of her head. She is wearing a white tee shirt that has blue dog tracks all over it, white knee-length overalls that have a blue flower pattern on them, white socks, and blue sneakers with small white flowers on them. The only incongruous touch is the fact that the sneakers are untied.

Inés begins her day working in her reading workbook. Each day the children have to finish all the pages that go with the story they read the previous day.

Inés spends almost an hour doing three workbook pages. Three times she asks the observer for assistance. In two cases she needs to know what a picture is so she can complete the exercise. The first time the picture shows a horse's hoof with the word *pe__ña* below it. It is only through looking at the choice of syllables and by the process of elimination that the observer is able to tell Inés that she is supposed to make it say *pezuña*. A picture of a mountain top is a little easier for the observer, but Inés does not seem to know the word *cima*. The third time, the directions for the workbook page are to underline the word that she hears, and she is sent to the teacher, who tells her not to do that page.

Inés does not work consistently in her workbook. While working, she also takes all her pencils out of her pencil case, counts them, puts them back, unsnaps the strap of her overalls, looks at her tee shirt, snaps the overalls again, stands up, puts one foot on her chair, then both feet on her chair, crouches on her toes while she works, looks at her workbook, picks it up and starts towards the teacher's desk, stops to talk to Nina, goes back and puts the workbook on her desk, joins Marisol and Evita, who are looking at the caterpillars on the science table, then finally gets her workbook again and brings it to the observer with another question about what to do. The page she is puzzled by has four sentences, each with a blank at the beginning of it. There are also four pictures on the page. She is supposed to write the word *Voy* (I'm going) on the blank in each sentence and then draw a line matching the sentence with the correct picture. Inés returns to her desk, but goes back to look at the caterpillars and a giant sea shell before sitting down and doing the task on the page.

Inés goes to the computer to write her daily journal entry. She writes a few words, then gets up and asks the classroom aide how to write something. Returning to the computer with a small slip of paper in her hand she writes some more, but is interrupted when the whole class goes to the library. On returning to the classroom, she goes right back to the computer, but is again interrupted to go to the computer room, where she works with a touch typing program. When she comes back from the computers she goes to her desk, seeming to forget that she hasn't finished her journal. But there are only a few minutes until recess anyway.

After recess, the student teacher does a mathematics lesson on money, then hands out a worksheet that the children do alone. Lunch follows, and after lunch Inés takes her math paper to the classroom aide to be checked. She leaves the math paper with the aide, then apparently remembers her unfinished journal, because she goes over to the computer and sits down again. The aide calls her back, however, to correct one problem on her math paper. She has confused the pictures of a dime and a penny, which were difficult to tell apart, and therefore gotten one problem wrong. Inés goes to her desk, corrects the problem, takes the paper back to the aide, and returns to her desk. The unfinished journal is again forgotten.

For the next ten minutes, Inés sits at her desk eating cereal that was shared by the group that had "bought" it during the math lesson, talking to Ignacio, and wiggling around. Then she gets her homework papers, puts her name on them, and puts them in her backpack. In the whole-class activity that follows, the children collaborate on composing a big book about Ángela. Ingrid's contribution is: *"Ella habla mucho."* ("She talks a lot.") She is still wiggling around, sitting with her feet on her chair, or sitting on her desk, and Matilde has to say to her,

| | |
|---|---|
| *"Baja las piernas allí, siéntate como debes."* | ("Put your legs down there, sit down like you're supposed to.") |

The day ends with the whole class listening to Ángela read a book she has written about Matilde. Ines's unfinished journal is still on the computer screen. It says:

Case Study, pp. 115.

| | |
|---|---|
| *Pasado ayer yo fui al cine con mi hermano y mi mama y mi papa y la pelicula que vimos fue* THE FLINTSTONES. | (The day after yesterday I went to the movies with my brother and my mom and my dad and the movie that we saw was THE FLINTSTONES.) |

*Observe a second grade child through a full day and compare his or her activities with those of one of the children in Matilde's room. What similarities and differences do you see? Give possible reasons for them.*

Observation

Authentic Purpose, pp. 67-72.

The journal that Inés began but never finished represents only a small portion of the writing done by the children in Matilde's class. The students spend a great deal of time writing, but neither are they enthusiastic about it, nor do they seem to do it easily. Matilde calls them "reluctant" writers. Their daily journals are often simple recitations of what they did the previous day:

| | |
|---|---|
| *Ayer yofui a la tienva acomprar gugo con tortitas con mi mama.* | (Yesterday Iwent to the stor tobuy guice with cookies with my mother.) |
| *yo fiu a new YorK. Yo vi a mi papá. y fiu a su casa.* | (i wnet to new YorK. I saw my father. and i wnet to his house.) |

The two children who had not gone to first grade do their journals through the **language experience approach**, although Ángela will later begin to write hers alone. Today Yoni takes his journal to Matilde. They talk about what he might want to write.

| | |
|---|---|
| *"¿Qué vas a escribir? ¿Cómo pasaste el fin de semana? ¿Cómo te portaste, bien o no? ¿Y tu hermana? ¿Una fiesta? ¿Gozaste* | ("What are you going to write? How did you spend the weekend? How did you behave, —well or not? And your sister? |

**20** • TEACHING BILINGUAL CHILDREN

*la fiesta? ¿Qué hiciste tú en la fiesta? ¿Y había amigos tuyos allí también?¿No conocías a nadie?"*

(a party? Did you enjoy the party? What did you do at the party? And were there friends of yours there too? You didn't know anybody?")

As Yoni answers her questions Matilde writes, neither reading aloud what she is writing nor directing his attention to the words on the paper. She asks him to read what she has written. He reads the first two words, stumbles on the third, and ends up repeating word for word as Matilde points to each word and reads it for him. He then goes back to his desk and copies into his journal what Matilde has written.

Other writing assignments are often very difficult for many of the children. Inés spends two hours thinking after writing the first sentence of a book about spring: *Ya biene la primabera.* (Sbring is now koming.) When asked why she hasn't written anything else, she explains that she can't think of anything to say about spring.

The children are expected to write four or five books for publication during the course of the year. Although Matilde often suggests other topics, most of the children write on seasonal themes such as fall, winter, Valentine's Day, spring, and Easter. Some children spend much of their free time writing drafts of books, but others need to be reminded, and there are days when Matilde asks everybody to work in their writing folders. The contents of the folder depend on where the child is in the writing process. Camilo has a stack of half-size sheets of newsprint in his folder because he's about to start a new book. It's the middle of February, and he's going to write a book about Valentine's Day. He takes out his ruler and draws two or three lines lengthwise across the bottom of one sheet of newsprint. Then he writes a sentence on the lines, lays his head on his arm and thinks for a while, writes some more, thinks some more, and writes again. He repeats this procedure for two more sheets of newsprint, puts them all in his folder, and puts the folder in his desk. The text that he has written looks like this:

la flor es bonita en el. DíA De san balenTín,

Hay un bosque Decorasones y Deramas

En El Dia DeSanbalenTín. dan cartas y chocolaTes.

(*thE flower is preTTy On. SAinT balenTine's dAy,
There is a foresT OfhearTs and Ofbranches
On sainTbalenTine'sDay. you give cards and chocolaTes.*)

A few days later, Camilo has a conference with Matilde. He begins reading his story, but is interrupted after two or three lines:

*"No tienes que poner un punto al final de cada línea, tienes que poner un punto al final de la*

("You don't have to put a period at the end of every line—you have to put a period

Investigations

List as many ways as you can think of to make writing easier for these children.

*oración.* at the end of the sentence.)

If you put a period when it isn't the end of a sentence, it's not a complete sentence. That sentence has no meaning."

Matilde now reads what Camilo wrote:

"*'la flor es bonita en el día* ("'the flower is pretty on
*de San Valentín.'* Saint Valentine's Day.')

Sentences begin with what kind of letter, Camilo?"

There is a pause as Matilde checks on Evita's math book and sends Teresa back to her seat to work in her reading workbook. Then the conference continues. "Is this a complete sentence? No, because it's going to continue here. Then why is there a period? Don't add things, Camilo, that you shouldn't do in writing. I taught you the rules of what you should do when you write, the form of writing.

*'Corazón,'* accent, *¿verdad que sí?* ('Heart,') accent, (right? 'of
*'De ramas...,' 'de ramas' son dos* branches...,' 'of branches' is
*palabras. No es una palabra."* two words. It's not one word.")

There is another pause as Matilde talks with Yoni about what he wants to write in his journal and writes down what he dictates. The conference continues.

"*¿Y qué va aquí? Punto. ¿Y* ("And what goes here? Period.
*porqué pusiste una mayúscula* And why did you put a capital
*aquí?"* letter here?")

Another pause as Matilde reminds Ángela's group that they should be working and not talking and Teresa that she has workbook pages she is supposed to be correcting. Then back to the conference. "*Dime lo que pasa aquí. Durante las páginas* ("Tell me what's happening here. On pages) one to four, I was correcting for you. Now you tell me what's happening here.

*Mayúscula, ¿eso debe ser qué? Si* (Capital letter, that should be
*no hay mayúscula, ¿tiene que ser* what? If it's not a capital letter,
*qué? Minúscula. Y espacio entre* it has to be what? Small letter.
*todas las palabras, ¿verdad que* And space between all the
*sí, Camilo? ¿Y aquí? 'El día de* words, right, Camilo? And here?
*San Valentín,' es oración con* 'On St. Valentine's Day,' is that
*sentido? No, es una frase. Ahora,* a sentence with meaning? No,
*si sacamos el punto, es una* it's a phrase. Now if we take
*oración hecha correctamente.* out the period, it's a correctly
*¿Verdad que sí?"* made sentence. Right?")

Pause as a child from another room comes in with a note for Matilde. She reads it, laughs, writes a response, and the child leaves. The conference continues. "*'En el día de San Valentín...' Corrige esa oración.*" ("'On Saint Valentine's Day...' Correct that sentence.") Camilo writes something and scratches his head.

Pause for Matilde to check the drawings Marisol has made for her book and to give Marisol a blue cardboard book cover to illustrate. Then Matilde says to Camilo, *"Chequea cada palabra, Camilo."* ("Check each word, Camilo.") Camilo begins to check his work.

*"Espacio. ¿Qué signo usamos cuando tenemos que dejar espacio? Esto quiere decir que tenemos que dejar un espacio entre una palabra y otra. Sigue con las palabras."*

("Space. What sign do we use when we have to leave a space? That means that we have to leave a space between one word and another. Go on with the words.")

Camilo continues checking his work. *"¿Por qué vas a poner una mayúscula allí, Camilo?"* ("Why are you going to put a capital letter there, Camilo?")

Pause as Jorge comes to talk to the teacher about his reading workbook. Matilde then looks back to Camilo.

*"Todavía no has terminado con la palabra 'fiesta.' Ahora 'en la.' Esas son correcciones que tú mismo puedes hacer. Mira cada página. Es una pena que estés escribiendo con tantos errores así. Esto está mal."*

("You still haven't finished with the word 'party.' Now 'in the.' Those are corrections that you can make yourself. Look at each page. It's a shame that you're writing with so many mistakes like that. This is bad.")

Pause to help Ángela with a math paper. Back to Camilo.

*"Despacio. Mayúscula. Minúscula. 'Lucy…' 'Lucy' es con la ce, aquí. ¿Qué es esta palabra aquí? ¿Cómo se escribe, Camilo? ¿Con qué? Esa es mayúscula que tienes allí, en mitad de la oración. ¿Eso es correcto? Aquí, ¿comb-b-brar, o comp-p-prar? ¿Qué tienes que usar para escribir la palabra 'comp-p-prar?' -p-p-rar. Comp-p-prar."*

("Slowly. Capital letter. Small letter. 'Lucy…' 'Lucy' is with a c here. What is this word here? How is it written, Camilo? With what? That's a capital letter that you have there, in the middle of the sentence. Is that correct? Here, *comb-b-brar*, or *comp-p-prar*? What do you have to use to write the word '*comp-p-prar?' -p-p-rar. Comp-p-prar*.")

All the corrections are now finished, and Camilo's first draft has arrows pointing at all the capital letters that should be small letters, vertical lines drawn where there should be spaces between words, and unneeded periods crossed off.

Matilde begins to write. She is copying onto white paper the text from the pages that she and Camilo have corrected. Camilo watches her write, blinking his eyes, frowning, shaking his head. Matilde says, *"En éste aquí, vamos a ver si podemos ponerlo así."* ("On this one here, let's see if we can put it like this.") She shows the page to him, saying, *"Así es como vamos a escribirlo."* ("This is how we're going to write it.") She writes some more, then reads, *"Los árboles*

Investigations

List other aspects of Camilo's story that might have been brought up in the writing conference.

La flor es bonita en el
día de San Valentín.

*(The flower is pretty on
Saint Valentine's day.)*

La casa de San Valentín.

*(The house of Saint Valentine.)*

Hay un bosque de
corazones. Los arboles tienen
muchas ramas.

*(There is a forest of hearts. The
trees have a lot of branches.)*

Hay unos pajaros de
corazones

*(There are some birds made
out of hearts.)*

Hay unos caramelos que
saben a chocolates

*(There are some candies that
taste like chocolates.)*

Hoy es día de San Valentín
en la escuela.

*(Today is Saint Valentine's
day in school.)*

En el día de San Valentín
dan cartas y chocolates.

*(On Saint Valentine's Day, you
give cards and chocolates.)*

Yo tuve una fiesta
en la escuela.

*(I had a party in school.)*

Yo le di una carta a Lucy.

*(I gave Lucy a card.)*

*tienen muchas ramas."* ("The trees have a lot of branches.")

When Camilo's book is finished, the text reads as shown on page 24. Each page is carefully illustrated, the front and back covers are laminated and taped together, and both the first draft and the final version are stapled inside the covers. The book will be placed in a bin where it will be available for other children to read in their spare time.

Matilde's classroom contains an abundance of material for the children to read in their spare time. Everywhere you look there is a shelf or a desk or a box or a crate full of books. Besides the student-published books, there are easy-to-read books in both English and Spanish, trade books arranged according to topic, commercial **big books** with sets of small books that go with them, and big books composed by Matilde's students in previous years. The atmosphere sends out a warm invitation to sit down in a quiet corner and explore the riches promised by this treasure of reading material. When children have finished their other work, they may get up and get books. They may also take books home through a check-out system that Matilde has devised. They often choose the predictable books that have been read to them in big book form. One of these **predictable books** is the only book that Yoni can read. They also like to read the published books written by their classmates. If they choose a book with which they're not familiar, they often just turn the pages, looking at the pictures without reading. Sometimes they get a book, take it to their desks, and then get up and put it back without even looking at it.

Reading instruction is done from copies of stories taken from a **basal reader** or from multiple sets of the same book. A small group of children who are all reading the same story join Matilde at the round table or at the listening center. They read aloud, discuss the story, complete story maps, and write responses to what they have read. They also do workbook pages. Sometimes Matilde works individually with certain students. There doesn't seem to be any particular schedule for when or with whom she does reading. Sometimes several days pass with no formal reading instruction at all.

During April, Matilde begins daily basal reading instruction. There are three reading groups that work out of the same primer-level Spanish basal reader, while the fourth reads from copies of a Spanish **pre-primer**, and works on phonics worksheets. Except for the fourth group, the groups are not ability-based. When asked why she reinstituted basal reading in a **whole language** classroom, Matilde replies, *"That was to hone in more on the comprehension, and to do more with them on that, because this group has been so teacher-dependent. When I ask inferential questions about what has been read and everything, it's like they just wait for me to say it for them, so I figured, well, let me start some reading groups here, and do a little more individual work so that when they finish reading, they can actually sit down and write the answers to the questions themselves. We were giving them reading sheets to do for comprehension, and even though they were very simple, a quick story, three or four paragraphs, they had a difficult time answering the questions about the story, and I think that the groups, and reading the story with them, and listening to them read, that they were able to think a little bit more about what they actually do when they read, what actually happens when you're reading, that you listen and you pay attention to details so you can actually answer back and tell what's going on."*

Investigations

Compare the first draft of Camilo's story (on p. 21) with the final version. What changes in form and content occurred? How did they occur?

The reading comprehension sheets that Matilde had been giving the children for homework are from a series called *Leyendo para comprender (Reading to Understand)*. They consist of three or four paragraphs describing something unusual about an animal, followed by seven questions including multiple choice, true/false, word definitions, synonyms and antonyms, and locating the paragraph in which specific information can be found. The format of the questions is similar to that found on **standardized tests** of reading comprehension.

---

*¿Puede una serpiente salir de un hoyo yendo para atrás?*

1 A veces vemos a una serpiente meterse en un hoyo muy chiquito. Parece que la serpiente es tan ancha como el hoyo. No creemos que pueda dar la vuelta. Nos preguntamos como podrá salir.

2 Si la serpiente entra en el hoyo de un animal, tal vez encuentre un buen lugar para dar la vuelta. Un animal a veces hace un cuartito al final de su hoyo. De fuera el hoyo parece pequeño. Pero puede ser más grande debajo de la tierra donde no podemos verlo. La serpiente va al cuartito y da la vuelta.

3 ¿Que pasa si la serpiente entra en un hoyo que no tiene un cuartito debajo de la tierra? El cuerpo de la serpiente la ayuda a salir del hoyo. Su cuerpo es largo y flaco. La serpiente puede doblarlo fácilimente. Da una vuelta completa y sale culebreando. Nadie ha visto a una serpiente salir de un hoyo yendo para atrás. Sale como entró—de cabeza.

1. Marca el cículo (○) al lado de la respuesta correcta. Nadie ha visto a una serpiente salir de un hoyo _____.
   ○ yendo para átras    ○ de cabeza    ○ como entró    ○ pequeño

2. El cuente no habla _____ la serpiente.
   ○ del cuerpo    ○ del color de    ○ de como da la vuelta
   ○ de los hoyos en que se mete

3. Escribe SÍ después de cada oracíon que es verdad. Escribe NO después de cada oración que no es verdad.
   Una serpiente nunca se mete en un hoyo pequeño. _____
   Una serpiente puede dar la vuelta en un cuartito debajo de la tierra. _____
   Una serpiente sale de un hoyo de cabeza. _____

4. Tacha la palabra que no va con las otras.
   dar          salir          ver          hoyo

5. Haz un círculo alrededor del número del párrafo 1 que habla del cuerpo de la serpiente.
   1               2               3

6. Escribe la palabra del párrafo 1 que significa <u>entrar</u> _____

7. ENTRAR es lo contrario de SALIR. <u>Gordo</u> es lo contrario de _____.
   ○ pequeño        ○ flaco        ○ largo        ○ grande

Leyendo para comprender                                    © 1974 The Continental Press, Inc.

Copyright 1974, The Continental Press, Inc. Used with permission.

*Can a snake go out of a hole backwards?*

1  *Sometimes we see a snake go into a very small hole. It seems as if the snake is as wide as the hole. We don't think it can turn around. We ask ourselves how it will be able to get out.*

2  *If the snake goes into an animal's hole, it might find a good place to turn around. Sometimes an animal makes a little room at the end of its hole. From outside the hole looks small. But it can be bigger under the ground where we can't see it. The snake goes to the little room and turns around.*

3    *What happens if the snake goes into a hole that doesn't have a little room under the ground? The body of the snake helps it to come out of the hole. Its body is long and thin. The snake can bend it easily. It turns completely around and slithers out. Nobody has seen a snake come out of a hole backwards. It comes out as it went in—head first.*

1. Mark the circle (O) next to the correct response. Nobody has seen a snake come out of a hole _____.

    O backwards    O head first    O as it went in    O that is small

2. The story does not talk about _____.

    O the body of the snake      O the color of the snake
    O how the snake turns around    O the holes the snake goes into

3. Write YES after each sentence that is true. Write NO after each sentence that is not true.

    A snake never goes into a small hole. _____
    A snake can turn around in a little room under the ground. _____
    A snake comes out of a hole head first. _____

4. Cross out the word that does not go with the others.

    give        go out        see        hole

5. Make a circle around the number of the paragraph that talks about the body of the snake.

    1        2        3

6. Write the word from paragraph 1 that means to **go in**. _____

7. GO IN is the opposite of GO OUT. **Fat** is the opposite of _____.

    O small    O thin    O long    O big

One day Matilde decides to go over the worksheet the children have done the previous evening because they had made a lot of mistakes on it. "What we're going to do is go over the homework you did last night. I'm concerned about the reading. You're still not reading to understand what you read. The questions are the same as what we do in reading group. They're questions about what you understand. We're going to take this work and read it together, and then we're going to answer the questions together." Matilde switches to Spanish and continues:

"*Yo quiero saber por qué Uds. no están haciendo el trabajo como deben de hacer. Yo siempre digo que tienen que hacer el trabajo para comprender. Esto es algo que Uds. tienen que leer para información. No es leer palabras para leer palabras ni de caminar rápido para terminar. Si están leyendo palabras así, así, así para terminar, se pierde el propósito para leer. Si tienen más de dos errores, quiere decir que no están comprendiendo.*

("I want to know why you guys aren't doing your work like you should do it. I always say that you have to do the work to understand. This is something that you have to read for information. It's not reading words just to read words, and it's not going fast in order to finish. If you're reading words like this, like this, like this in order to finish, you lose the reason for reading. If you have more than two mistakes, that means that you're not understanding.)

"*¿Cuántos párrafos hay?*" ("How many paragraphs are there?") Several students answer "*Tres*" or "Three." The paragraphs are numbered on the paper.

| | |
|---|---|
| "*Sabemos que hay tres párrafos porque están indentados. En el primer párrafo, ¿cuántas oraciones hay?*" | ("We know that there are three paragraphs because they're indented. In the first paragraph, how many sentences are there?") |

Clarisa answers "*Siete.* (Seven.)" Seven is the number of questions that come after the story.

| | |
|---|---|
| "*Yo dije oraciones, no dije preguntas. Clarisa, ¿no sabes la diferencia entre una oración y una pregunta? Vamos a ver quién puede leer el primer párrafo. Vamos a poner atención. Evita.*" | ("I said sentences, I didn't say questions. Clarisa, don't you know the difference between a sentence and a question? Let's see who can read the first paragraph. Let's pay attention. Evita.") |

Evita begins to read the first paragraph. Matilde interrupts her just after she begins reading. "Excuse me, Evita.

| | |
|---|---|
| *Yo veo que parte del problema nuestro es que no hacemos lo que yo digo. Cuando una persona está leyendo, no estamos mirando por toda la clase. Estamos mirando las palabras. Sigue, Evita.*" | (I see that part of our problem is that we don't do what I say. When somebody is reading, we aren't looking around the classroom. We're looking at the words. Go on, Evita.") |

Evita continues reading.

"*OK, ¿quién quiere leer la segunda? OK, Teresa.*" ("OK, who wants to read the second one? OK, Teresa.") Teresa reads.

"*Ya terminaste? OK. El tercer párrafo allí. Clarisa.*" ("Did you finish? OK. The third paragraph there. Clarisa.") Clarisa reads only the first sentence before Matilde interrupts with "*Esa es una pregunta,*" ("That's a question,") and rereads it with question intonation. Clarisa continues reading.

Matilde interrupts again. "*Hay puntos allí, mijita. Tienes que parar allí.*" ("There are periods there, honey. You have to stop there.") Matilde rereads the sentences, stopping conspicuously at each period.

"*¿Quién quiere terminar ese parrafo allí, por favor? Inés.*" ("Who wants to finish that paragraph there, please? Inés.") Inés reads, needing help only on the word *culebreando.*

After the three paragraphs of the story have been read aloud, Matilde asks a few literal comprehension questions in Spanish: What did we read about? What's the snake's body like? Did the story talk about the color of the snake? Can the snake bend? Has anybody seen a snake come out of a hole backwards? She then goes over the questions on the worksheet, eliciting answers to each of

Investigations

Discourse Analysis, p. 115.

them and having the children tell which paragraph contains the sentence that gives the answer to the question. If a student suggests the wrong paragraph, Matilde simply tells him or her to keep looking. Some of the children pay attention, check to be sure they have the correct answer before volunteering, and correct their worksheets. Others volunteer, but seem to be guessing at answers. Still others aren't paying much attention at all. (A complete transcript of this session is included in the Appendix.)

After seeing that the children are having difficulty doing these reading comprehension worksheets, Matilde institutes basal reading groups. From April until the end of the year she meets with each of the reading groups every day, reading one story a day from the basal reader and having the children do the corresponding workbook pages as seatwork. She explains about the books and the workbooks during the first meeting with one of the groups.

*"OK, ¿qué más grupo iba a coger hoy?* ("OK, what other group was I going to take today?) Can I have your group please, Nina?" Nina, Nicolás, Jaime, Julio, and Clarisa go to the listening center.

| | |
|---|---|
| *"¿Uds. no han leído de este libro? Vamos a empezar en la página nueve."* | ("You guys haven't read from this book? We're going to start on page nine.") |

Matilde reads word for word from the introductory page of the story:

| | |
|---|---|
| *"'Preparación para la lectura. Sílabas abiertas: rra, rre, rri, rro, rru; gorra, carreta, perrito, carro, serrucho.' Estamos en la página diez. 'Palabras nuevas: corre, correcaminos, carrera, perrito, corro, baile, conejo.'"* | ("'Preparation for reading. Open syllables: rra, rre, rri, rro, rru; cap, cart, puppy, car, saw.' We're on page ten. 'New words: run, roadrunner, race, puppy, I run, dance, rabbit.'") |

The words that Matilde reads have pictures to illustrate their meaning. There is no discussion of them, although a previous group reading the same story discussed some of them. As Julio begins reading the first page of the story, Matilde calls to Yoni to bring his journal to her. She looks at it, sees that he has done it, and sends him for his reading folder. The children in the reading group continue reading aloud in order, two pages at a time. The story is called *"A los tres nopales"* (literally, "To the Three Cacti"). There has been no discussion of the title, although these urban children from the northeastern part of the United States are unlikely to know what a *nopal* is.

The children read word for word, with little intonation to show that they understand what they are reading and with some trouble decoding some of the words. While Clarisa is reading, Matilde gets up and goes to check on what some of the other children are doing at their seats. She isn't there when Clarisa finishes, but Jaime goes on reading without being told to do so.

The story is interrupted by lunch. When the children return, they begin where they left off. When the children have finished reading the story, Matilde reads verbatim the four questions that are printed in the book at the end of the story:

| | |
|---|---|
| *"¿Qué animal es el más rápido del campo? ¿Qué hace el conejo para ganar la carrera? ¿Por qué no ganan el perro y el correcaminos? ¿Cómo crees que se sentía el conejo al ganar la carrera?"* | ("What animal is the fastest of the countryside? What does the rabbit do to win the race? Why don't the dog and the road-runner win? How do you think the rabbit felt when he won the race?") |

The children's answers are so soft that they are unintelligible. They are also short, and there is no further discussion of the story, although the previous group talked a little bit about the rabbit cheating. Matilde then takes a stack of workbooks off the shelf behind her, saying, *"OK, son sus libros."* ("OK, these are your books.") "In this book here

| | |
|---|---|
| *se puede trabajar solamente cuando hemos terminado el cuento. Ahora terminanos el primer cuento.* | (you can only work when we have finished the story. Now we finished the first story.) |

Open your books please.

| | |
|---|---|
| *Ahora se puede trabajar en las páginas dos, tres, cuatro, cinco; página seis no.* | (Now you can work on pages two, three, four, five; page six no.) |

Follow along so you'll know what to do. That's why I'm doing this, for your benefit.

| | |
|---|---|
| *'Los tres nopales' empieza aquí. ¿Por qué no se puede hacer la página seis? ¿Leímos el cuentito 'La carrera'? No. ¿Cómo se llama el cuento que leímos nosotros? 'Los tres nopales.' Los animales hicieron una carrera, pero no estaba titulado 'La carrera.'* | ('The Three Nopales' begins here. Why can't you work on page six? Did we read the story 'The Race?' No. What's the name of the story that we read? 'The Three Nopales.' The animals had a race, but it wasn't called 'The Race.') |

You will always bring the book to me and we will do the correction of the pages and everything."

These are the only instructions the children receive about what to do on their workbook pages. They are expected to read the directions on each page and do it independently.

Investigations

Observation

*Observe a writing conference or a reading group and compare it to the one described here. What similarities and differences are there? Give some possible reasons for them.*

The children are also expected to read the directions on the pages of their mathematics books and do them independently. Although the children work in their math books every day, Matilde seldom teaches whole-class mathematics lessons. This may be because, as she claims, the students don't pay attention to whole-class lessons very well. It may also be because she has never had mathematics books for the whole class. She says that she orders math books every year, but *"they always take my order, and when I come back in September, they say, 'Oh, well, we had to cut, and your order was one of the ones we cut.' I say, 'Well, what a surprise. You always cut my order—always.' I've never had a series of math books. If I ever get a series of math books I'll be so happy, I think I'll sing and dance."*

Learn by Doing, pp. 73-79.

This year all the children have their own math books, but they're all different. *"I had done an evaluation of different math series in September. As part of it, I was able to keep those books, so I had different math books from different series. I didn't have any two books that were alike, so all my kids have different math books. So when I work with the kids, it's like 'OK, you don't have the same book. Well, you're going to work on this page here.' It begins to be a hassle, some books are better than other books, some of them have a lot of the skills that you want to teach. I look at some of the masters that I have and see if I can get some enrichment activities and stuff, but I can't say 'OK everybody, turn to page 1-0-2.' So you look at them individually, 'So-and-so, you do this page.' That part of it can become kind of tiresome."*

The children work in their math books every morning after they have written in their journals and completed any other work they have been assigned for that particular day. It's not clear how they know what pages to do. Instruction is provided in various ways. Sometimes Matilde circulates while the children are working in their math books, watching them work and giving help where needed.

> *"¿Cuántos hay en total? Aquí no es quitar, tienes que sumar. 'En total,'*
>
> ("How many are there in all? Here it's not subtraction; you have to add. 'In all,')

all together. You did this one fine. What happened over here? I want those two corrected."

Sometimes a child working in a math book approaches Matilde with a question while Matilde is doing something else. Sometimes that child gets help. Sometimes she is told, "Not now." Sometimes Matilde calls a child to her desk to give feedback as she is correcting math books or homework. That's how Omar and Nicolás learn to check subtraction by adding: "Omar, come here for a second. Nicolás, can I see you too? Come here, I'll show you how to add to check your subtraction. See, I add these two lines, three plus one is four. But this number is nine, so something is wrong. I add this right here, seven plus five is twelve. Is this the same as this number? So is this right? No. That's how I find out that it's wrong."

Sometimes Matilde demonstrates math in action as she helps the children figure out if they have enough money to order the books they want from the paperback book club: "This one is 95 cents, and this one is 50 cents. How much is that? Do you have enough money? No? How much more do you need? Let's write a note to your mother.

| | |
|---|---|
| *'Evita necesita cuarenta centavos más para comprar los libros que quiere. Me dio $2.05, y cuestan $2.45.' "* | ('Evita needs forty cents more to buy the books that she wants. She gave me $2.05, and they cost $2.45.'") |

She reads the note aloud as she writes it, all in Spanish except the last sum of money, which is read in English.

Sometimes, if the whole class is having trouble with the same thing, Matilde writes problems on the board and has students work through them out loud. This happens one day when the majority of the students have done their subtraction homework without regrouping. She puts a problem from the homework on the board:

$$546$$
$$- 73$$

and asks Nicolás to do it. Nicolás goes to the board and writes 533. Matilde looks at the answer and says, "Let's check that. Remember how I taught you to add in order to check your subtraction? Draw your line to show that you're going to add." Nicolás writes a plus sign, draws a line, and adds 73 and 533. Matilde walks over to the board and draws a line from the sum Nicolás has just written, 606, to the top number of the problem, 546. *"¿Esos son iguales? ¿No? Entonces está mal."* ("Are those the same? No? Then it's wrong.") Turning to the class, she continues, *"Clase, ¿qué pasa aquí en decenas?"* ("Class, what happens here in the tens?") When several students answer "Regroup" in English, she continues in English. "We have to regroup. We go to the hundreds, *a las centenas*. We have to borrow, so we need to regroup." Nicolás redoes the problem, this time with regrouping. "OK, let's add again and make sure how this is going to end up. Remember we always go back to the ones column to start to add. Is that correct, Nicolás? Remember that you can check your own work."

Several more students do similar problems correctly after they have been reminded about regrouping. When it is Julio's turn he does his problem correctly, but he has trouble explaining what he has done. His problem is:

$$961$$
$$- 237$$

and he begins with: *"Siete menos uno, no se puede. Quitamos uno…"* ("Seven minus one, can't be done. We take one…") Matilde interrupts, "Wait a minute, I'm not understanding anything you're saying. I don't understand.

| | |
|---|---|
| *Explícame. ¿Estamos quitando o estamos sumando? ¿Qué es el proceso?"* | (Explain it to me. Are we subtracting or are we adding? What's the process?") |

Julio replies that it's subtraction.

**Investigations**

List activities that students could do to help them remember when they have to regroup.

"All right, *comienza con la primera columna allí. ¿Cuál es? ¿Cuál es la primera columna? ¿Es la columna de qué?*" ("All right, (begin with the first column there. Which one is it? Which is the first column? It's the column of what?")

Julio finally understands the question and responds, *"Unidades."* ("Ones.") Matilde continues, *"Unidades ahora. Uno quita siete. ¿Puedes?"* ("Ones now. One take away seven. Can you do it?") Julio replies, *"No."* "What do you have to do?" *"Reagrupar."* ("Regroup.")

*"¿Reagrupaste ya? Pero no dijiste nada a nosotros. ¿Qué vas a reagrupar? Sigue allí por favor."* ("Did you already regroup? But you didn't say anything to us. What are you going to regroup? Go on there, please.")

Although Julio has done the problem correctly, he can't explain how he did it. His round face often shows a look of not quite understanding what's going on; that look is now intensified. Combining both the regrouping and the subsequent subtraction in the tens column into one operation, he blurts out, *"Seis menos uno quedan dos."* ("Six minus one leaves two.") He then hurries through the hundreds column and on to his attempt to add to show that the problem was correct. *"Nueve menos dos son siete. Siete más nueve…"* ("Nine minus two is seven. Seven plus nine…")

Matilde interrupts. "I think you're losing us, Julio.

*Tú vas para Chicago dejando a nosotros acá. Vamos a seguir con nueve quita dos.* (You're going to Chicago and leaving us behind here. Let's continue with nine take away two.)

Do you know where we are? *Nueve quita dos.*" (Nine take away two.")

Julio repeats, *"Nueve quita dos quedan siete."* ("Nine take away two leaves seven.")

Matilde asks, "So what's the answer?" and Julio responds in English, "Seven hundred twenty-four."

"What is it in Spanish," she asks.

*"Siete mil…,"* ("Seven thousand…,") which is interrupted by the exclamation,

*"¡¿Siete mil?! We haven't started the millares yet. ¿Cuál estamos estudiando?"* ("Seven thousand?!) We haven't started the (thousands) yet. (What are we studying?")

Julio answers, *"Centenas."* (Hundreds.")

*"Centenas.* (Hundreds.) So *¿siete qué?* (seven what?) Who can help him? Mariana?"

Mariana goes to the board and says, *"Setecientos veinticuatro."* ("Seven hundred twenty-four.") Julio repeats the number in Spanish, heaves a sigh of relief, and sits down, tripping over his untied shoe lace as he does so. A little light on the heel of one of his sneakers blinks on and off each time he steps on it. The untied sneaker doesn't blink.

Julio seems to enjoy science classes much more than mathematics. Science is taught in English by a specialist teacher so Julio's English proficiency helps him. There is very little written work involved, so his inability to sit and work quietly does not hinder him as it does in math.

One day Mr. Goodwin, the science teacher, walks into Matilde's room at science time with a plastic cup in his hand. He shows it to the children and asks them what's in it. "Caterpillars!" comes the nearly unanimous response. "And what happens to caterpillars when they grow up?" "Butterflies!" comes the chorus from the children.

Mr. Goodwin has talked with the children previously about life cycles of moths and butterflies. Now they review what they have learned. He shows a book, saying, "This says *Butterflies and Moths*. I get confused. What's the difference? Who remembers? How are we going to know which is which?"

Nicolás answers. "The moth, it has the body of a circle."

Mr. Goodwin draws a circle on the board to represent a moth, and then adds an oval for a butterfly body. Marisol comments, "And then the antennas, on the oval, it's curvy. On the butterfly it's not curvy."

Mr. Goodwin draws appropriate antennae on each body, even though Marisol mixed up ovals and circles, or perhaps butterflies and moths. "Something else is different," he adds.

Omar responds, "The moth flies at night."

"You're right, now I'm remembering," says Mr. Goodwin. "Some other things, too, you're doing great."

Nina volunteers, "It looks like someone's got a computer, it gots a little button, and when you use it, it goes like that," going to the blackboard and drawing a picture of a box with an extended antenna on it.

Mr. Goodwin ignores her confusion about butterfly antennae and television antennas, and continues, "Let's see if I can remember about the life cycle of these animals." He writes "butterfly" and "moth" on the board, reading them aloud as he writes. "When we talked about this before, I told you that I ordered some butterflies and they sent me something that didn't look like a butterfly."

The children chorus, "Caterpillars," and Iris adds, "Yea, you put them in cocoons and they turn into butterflies." Iris is a large girl, several heads taller than anybody else in the room, and quite chubby. She often interrupts to make comments that show her lack of understanding.

Mr. Goodwin draws a caterpillar under each heading on the board and labels them both "larva." "What was a caterpillar before it was a caterpillar?" Without waiting for an answer, he draws and labels an egg under each heading. "I can't tell the difference between these two," he says.

Nina gets up and draws something unrecognizable on the board, talking about eggs getting bigger and something she had seen in a book. Iris repeats that you put the caterpillar in a cocoon.

Mr. Goodwin continues. "There's something about a cocoon. This animal, the moth, spins a cocoon around itself. What about the butterfly? Does it spin a cocoon?"

Nina picks up the *Butterflies and Moths* book and shows Mr. Goodwin one picture in which the eggs are little and another in which the eggs are big. He explains that those are just different pictures. Then he takes the book and looks at it, commenting as he does, "Let me see if there's something different about the butterfly. This says 'cocoon' for the moth, but over here it says 'chrysalis.' They're different. Remember, the butterfly attaches itself to the top. The butterfly can go anywhere. If you see a cocoon around it, you know it's a moth. The moth sort of spins this cocoon around itself, but what the butterfly does, it goes up and sort of splits itself and hangs there."

Returning to the board and drawing, he continues, "So we call this one a pupa. Then it becomes an adult." He adds an adult to each set of drawings, which now form a circle. "Then they die. Then they're all gone. But first they lay eggs, so we're going around again, like a cycle."

"How about the colors?" he asks. A child responds, "Moths are like just white, just big and white," and Mr. Goodwin adds, "There's different colored moths, some of them are very pretty. Also I remember something about the wings. Some of them are sort of up like this, on their backs, and some of them just lay flat. What's this one?" He leans over and holds his arms out behind his back, and they take on a remarkable resemblance to a butterfly's wings. "What's this one?" Now he has turned into a moth, with his "wings" out to the side. The children guess wrong as to which is which. "No, it's the other way around, but it's good that you remembered."

They have indeed remembered a great deal from their previous lesson. Before he leaves, Mr. Goodwin puts the plastic cup on the science center table. It has five caterpillars in it and a layer of mush on the bottom of the cup.

The days pass and nothing happens to the caterpillars, except that they seem a little larger. Matilde occasionally reminds the children that they are there: "Have you guys been looking at the caterpillars? Remember that you can use the magnifying glass to see them, but don't knock them down."

One day another child accuses Rosita of killing one of the caterpillars by shaking the cup. Matilde demands,

| | |
|---|---|
| *"¿Cómo ella lo mató? Rosita, ¿cómo tú lo haces así? Eso no es para hacer así, para menearlo, es para mirar solamente."* | ("What do you mean she killed it? Rosita, why did you do that? That's not for that, for shaking it, it's only to look at.)" |

A group of children has gathered at the science center, discussing whether the caterpillar is indeed dead or not. "Matilde, come here, it's turning into a cocoon," Fernando calls. Another contradicts him: *"Ese está muerto."* ("That one's dead.") Matilde solves the controversy by pronouncing, *"No está muerto, está haciendo su capullo."* ("It's not dead, it's making its cocoon.") She must have felt some doubt however, because later in the day Mr. Goodwin comes in to check on the caterpillars and reminds the children not to shake the cup, or even to pick it up, or the chrysalis will fall down.

A week later there are two chrysalises and three caterpillars in the cup. The chrysalises are hanging down from the lid of the cup. Mr. Goodwin puts the cup into a large cardboard butterfly box, with plastic windows on three sides so the children can see inside. He tapes the lid of the cup to the inside top of the box. Anticipation mounts as the days pass and the remaining three caterpillars

Investigations

List activities the children could do to reinforce their knowledge of moths and butterflies.

change into chrysalises. Then one day there are two butterflies flying around inside the box, and the next day there are five. Mr. Goodwin puts them into a butterfly tower, a large cylinder of green nylon netting suspended from the ceiling over the science table. He gives them sugar water for food, and puts a plant inside the netting with them. He says the plant is for them to lay eggs on. When the eggs hatch, the caterpillars will eat the plant. He hopes the children will be able to observe the complete life cycle of the butterflies.

Unfortunately, time runs out before the butterflies lay any eggs. School is almost over for the summer, and one day, five painted lady butterflies are released into the school yard.

Some of the other science topics Mr. Goodwin covers with Matilde's children are heat and cold, magnets, the sun and the moon, food groups, growth, dinosaurs, and fossils. He also brings in baby chickens that were hatched in another classroom so the children can hold them. Matilde likes the way he connects his science teaching to what she is doing with the children in the classroom. When he is teaching about the phases of the moon, for example, he connects this topic to their social studies unit on Native Americans by reading the children a Native American legend about the moon.

The Native American unit has been going on for a long time. Matilde introduced it by reading a Native American legend to the children and asking them what they knew about Native Americans. She asked the children, "Do you believe there really are Indians that exist today *como de antes? ¿Que llevan la misma ropa?*" ("like before? Who wear the same clothing?") Ángela, dressed in a light blue skirt with winter scenes on it, lace tights and patent leather shoes, but looking as if she could be wearing the colorful woven clothing of a Mayan village, answered, *"No hay indios hoy en día."* ("There are no Indians nowadays.")

Since that introduction to the unit, the children have listened to many books having to do with Native Americans in both traditional and contemporary settings. They have learned about native crafts, wigwams, and pow wows. They have tasted fried Native American dough with maple syrup. They have made totem poles, drums, Eskimo prints, buckskins, and an Indian village diorama. A display on the blackboard tells them that "hickory," "moccasin," "wigwam," "totem," "squash," and "toboggan" are Native American words, as are "kayak," "Texas," "Lake Huron," "Miami," "Iowa," and "Niagra [sic] Falls."

It is now time for the culmination of the Native American unit. The children are sitting at their desks, listening to the soft sound of Native American chanting coming from the tape recorder in the listening center.

"If you made a drum, go and get it, " Matilde says. Eight of the children get up, go to the listening center table, and pick up the drums they made out of coffee cans the previous week. They take them back to their seats and begin to tap them softly in time to the chanting.

"Does someone want to play the maracas? There are three." Five children get up and start toward the bookshelves by the door. Two of them realize that the others will get there before they do; they turn around and go back to their seats. There is no running to beat somebody else to the maracas, nor any complaining about not getting a turn to use them. The soft swish of the maracas joins the quiet beat of the drums and the gentle murmur of the recorded chant.

**Investigations**

List as many ways as you can think of to introduce a unit on Native Americans.

"Do you have your chant sheets? We're going to do the Navajo prayer chant, OK? Those of you who have the maracas, I do not want you shaking them very hard." Papers appear on the children's desks. The teacher begins to chant in time to the music, and the children join in.

> *"Máy I wálk in beáuty befóre me,*
> *Máy I wálk in beáuty behínd me,*
> *Máy I wálk in beáuty abóve me,*
> *Máy I wálk in beáuty belów me,*
> *Whére there's beáuty áll aroúnd me,*
> *Máy I wálk."*

The chant is repeated, and the teacher announces that it is now time for the naming ceremony. "When I call you, I want you to come up and get your name and put it on your desks, and that will be your official Native American name." She takes a laminated sentence strip from the pile on the desk in front of her. The strip has a name and a series of pictographs on it. "Starface," she says. Julio gets up and takes the sentence strip.

Matilde calls the children one by one. "The Quiet One." This is an apt name for Diara. "Talking Rabbit." Marisol does talk a lot. "Sitting Bull." Jorge spends more time wandering around the room than sitting. "Dancing Flower." Rosita is a flower, a lovely flower unfolding in Matilde's garden. "Still Water." Liana does not know the saying "Still waters run deep," but it is appropriate for this quiet, intelligent child. "She Who Doesn't Know." Is that the image Mariana has of herself? "Lonesome Arrow." Is this a positive or a negative image for Ignacio?

The naming continues, accompanied by the soft beat of the drums and swish of the maracas. "Whispering Wind." "Singing Dove." "Running Deer." "Shining Moon." "Little Fish." After all the children have received their name strips, it's quiet for a moment. Then Julio pipes up, "What's your name, Matt?" The teacher turns to him, grins, and says, "Yelling Bear."

After the naming ceremony, the children tape their sentence strips with their new names to their desks. Marisol says, "Matilde, what's your name again?" "Yelling Bear!" she answers, pretending to yell. A bear, yes, definitely a bear. A large, brown mother bear, protective of her 25 cubs, but willing to cuff them when they step out of line. Guiding, teaching, lecturing, punishing, but very seldom yelling.

*Observe a mathematics, science, or social studies lesson and compare it to the one described here. Give possible reasons for any similarities and differences you find.*

---

It is difficult to deduce a consistent underlying approach to teaching and learning from the eclectic mix of activities in Matilde's classroom. This has been a whole language school for the last three years, and Matilde says she had been using a **whole language** approach for two or three years before that. She has taken courses in whole language and worked with consultants as she changed from her previous, more traditional teaching. She explains her own teaching:

Case Study, p. 116.

Observation

Beliefs, pp. 80-85.

**Investigations**

Discuss with a colleague which of Matilde's practices are consistent with a whole language approach.

*"What I do with whole language is to really hone in on spelling, on grammar, and not just present it to them, but we actually work on those things. Some people I think are still a little confused about how you implement whole language. We do a lot of spelling, we do the grammar, and writing paragraphs, and they write the different books. They get a chance to experience from the beginning, from September up until now, the length of the sentences that they write, the quality of the sentences. But it still requires a lot of encouraging, because you get those resistant writers. I like to think that we're doing a good job; that's what I've been told."*

| | MONDAY | | | TUESDAY | | | WEDNESDAY | | | THURSDAY | | | FRIDAY | |
|---|---|---|---|---|---|---|---|---|---|---|---|---|---|---|
| Min. | SUBJECT | From to | Min. | SUBJECT | From to | Min. | SUBJECT | From to | Min. | SUBJECT | From to | Min. | SUBJECT | From to |
| 15 | U.S.S.R | 9:20 | 15 | U.S.S.R | 9:20 | 15 | U.S.S.R | 9:20 | 15 | U.S.S.R | 9:20 | 15 | U.S.S.R | 9:20 |
| | | 9:35 | | | 9:35 | | | 9:35 | | | 9:35 | | | 9:35 |
| 45 | Math | 9:40 | 45 | Library | 9:40 | 45 | Math | 9:40 | 45 | Math | 9:40 | 45 | Math | 9:40 |
| | | 10:25 | | | 10:25 | | | 10:25 | | | 10:25 | | | 10:25 |
| 40 | Rdg/LngArts | 10:30 | 40 | Computer | 10:30 | 40 | Science | 10:30 | 40 | Computer | 10:30 | 40 | Rdg/LngArts | 10:30 |
| | | 11:10 | | | 11:10 | | | 11:10 | | | 11:10 | | | 11:10 |
| 40 | Rdg/LngArts | 11:15 | 40 | Rdg/LngArts | 11:15 | 40 | Rdg/LngArts | 11:15 | 40 | Rdg/LngArts | 11:15 | 40 | Rdg/LngArts | 11:15 |
| | | 11:55 | | | 11:55 | | | 11:55 | | | 11:55 | | | 11:55 |
| | RECESS 12:00 - 12:15 | | | RECESS | | | RECESS | | | RECESS | | | RECESS | |
| 10 | Rdg/LngArts | 12:20 | 10 | Rdg/LngArts | 12:20 | 10 | Rdg/LngArts | 12:20 | 10 | Rdg/LngArts | 12:20 | 10 | Rdg/LngArts | 12:20 |
| | | 12:30 | | | 12:30 | | | 12:30 | | | 12:30 | | | 12:30 |
| 45 | Science | 12:35 | 45 | Rdg/LngArts | 12:35 | 45 | Rdg/LngArts | 12:35 | 45 | Rdg/LngArts | 12:35 | 45 | Rdg/LngArts | 12:35 |
| | | 1:20 | | | 1:20 | | | 1:20 | | | 1:20 | | | 1:20 |
| | | | | | | | | | | | | | | |
| | 1:25 - 2:05 | | | | | | LUNCH PERIOD | | | | | | | |
| Min. | SUBJECT | From to | Min. | SUBJECT | From to | Min. | SUBJECT | From to | Min. | SUBJECT | From to | Min. | SUBJECT | From to |
| 30 | SocSt./ESL | 2:10 | 30 | SocSt./ESL | 2:10 | 30 | SocSt./ESL | 2:10 | 30 | SocSt./ESL | 2:10 | 30 | SocSt./ESL | 2:10 |
| | | 2:40 | | | 2:40 | | | 2:40 | | | 2:40 | | | 2:40 |
| 10 | D.E.A.R | 2:45 | 10 | D.E.A.R | 2:45 | 10 | D.E.A.R | 2:45 | 10 | D.E.A.R | 2:45 | 10 | D.E.A.R | 2:45 |
| | | 2:55 | | | 2:55 | | | 2:55 | | | 2:55 | | | 2:55 |
| | Dismissal | 3:00 | | Dismissal | 3:00 | | Dismissal | 3:00 | | Dismissal | 3:00 | | Dismissal | 3:00 |

Matilde's approach to scheduling is as eclectic and flexible as her approach to teaching. Her formal schedule, hanging on the wall behind her desk, includes time for mathematics, reading and language arts, sustained silent reading (Uninterrupted Sustained Silent Reading and Drop Everything and Read are times when everybody in the classroom is supposed to do nothing but read; although both of these were on the schedule, neither was actually done in Matilde's room), ESL, social studies, science, and computers. Only science, library, computer, recess, lunch, and dismissal occur at the times indicated, however. The rest of the time Matilde ignores the schedule. This creates a very relaxed feeling in the classroom, and also makes it possible to do projects that take up more time than would be allotted to a single subject on the schedule.

Although Matilde's approach to teaching is eclectic, her approach to student work habits is consistent. The ability to sit at one's desk and do work is important. Finishing that work is important. Finishing it neatly, completely, and correctly is important. Being quiet, listening, paying attention, and following directions are important. Doing homework is important. Doing it neatly, completely, and correctly is important.

The importance of learning to do work is shown by watching Matilde's interactions with Ángela and Yoni. Their most important task each day is to write in their journals, which they do through a **language experience** approach, copying what they have first dictated to the teacher or the aide. Then they are supposed to work from their folders, which contain miscellaneous phonics worksheets, math papers, and other seatwork. Matilde has to constantly remind Yoni, "*¿Tu folder? ¿Dónde está? ¡Sácalo!*" ("Your folder? Where is it? Get it out!")

Although Yoni does not make much progress in literacy development during the year, Ángela does. At the end of the year she can write in her journal without having to dictate to the teacher, and she reads simple books quite fluently. However, she also has to learn to sit and do work. When Ángela asks Matilde if she may read, the reply is,

"*No, tú no puedes leer, tienes que*  ("No, you can't read, you have
*hacer tus hojas de matemáticas.*"  to do your math sheets.")

When Ángela tries to show that she can read a book that's on her desk, Matilde replies, "*Guarda eso y saca el diario.*" ("Put that away and get out your journal.") On another day, the journal is also more important than a book she is reading: "What are you doing?

*¿Has hecho el diario? Saca el*  (Have you done your journal?
*diario,* miss. *Devuelve ese libro*  Get out your journal,) miss.
*donde pertenece.*"  (Put that book back where it
            belongs.")

When another adult in the classroom asks Ángela to bring a book and show how she can read, Matilde says, "She has work that she's supposed to be doing."

Finishing projects is important. When art creations are displayed, every child in the room must have one. Ángela had been absent on the March day when the rest of the class made leprechauns with large shamrock faces, accordion-folded arms and legs, and small shamrock hands and feet. On the day she returns Ángela spends the whole day, except for science and math lessons taught in English, making her leprechaun.

Homework is very important. The children have at least three pages of homework every day: spelling words, mathematics, and a reading worksheet. The aide checks the homework every morning, and anything that is wrong must be corrected. Children who don't bring in their homework are reminded to do so, and a tally of completed homework is kept for use in determining grades. The importance of doing the homework, and of doing it neatly, carefully, and correctly, is emphasized over and over.

There is also a lot of emphasis on correctness in the children's journal writing, correctness of both writing and the drawings that must accompany each entry. When Ángela brings her journal to show what she has written, Matilde's response is,

"*¿No te dije que no escribimos*  ("Didn't I tell you that we don't
*con mayúscula entre las palabras?*  write capital letters in the middle

| | |
|---|---|
| *Si no es el principio de una oración, o el nombre de alguien, no usamos mayúscula, usamos minúscula."* | of words? If it isn't the beginning of a sentence, or someone's name, we don't use capital letters, we use small letters.") |

She then continues with a comment on the picture Ángela has drawn:

| | |
|---|---|
| *"Tienes que coger tu crayola, y lo vas a hacer así, llenar todos los espacios, estamos en segundo grado ahora. Y la cara de la persona no es verde. ¿Tú tienes la cara verde? No.* | ("You have to take your crayon, and you're going to do it like this, filling all the spaces; we're in second grade now. And the person's face is not green. Do you have a green face? No. |

So I want to see you doing it like this, and like this. *Vamos."* (Let's go.")

At other times the emphasis may be on the amount of writing the children do in their journals. They are supposed to write four sentences each day, and one day when Matilde checks Camilo's journal, he has written only one sentence. *"¿Qué es eso? ¿Cuántas oraciones hay?* ("What is that? How many sentences are there?) This is poor. This is very poor. *¿Qué es eso?* (What is that?) Why are these words written together? What is this? What is all of this? I'm talking about your bad spelling and not completing the diary. And one sentence? How many sentences are you supposed to write in your journals? The minimum is four sentences, right? A paragraph. Is this a paragraph? Erase that and start over."

When the children make mistakes, they are often reminded that these are things they were supposed to have learned previously, things that Matilde has already taught them. "You've forgotten everything; *esto no es aceptable; comienza otra vez."* (this is not acceptable; start over again.") "What does 'paragraph' mean? What have we been studying? Have you forgotten?"

| | |
|---|---|
| *"No quiero ver las palabras mal escritas. Estudiamos la palabra 'bicicleta,' no sé cuántas veces."* | ("I don't want to see words written wrong. We studied the word 'bicycle,' I don't know how many times.") |

At times there is praise for journal writing, but not without first correcting misspelled words.

| | |
|---|---|
| *"'La otra…' sin hache, 'otra' es 'otra' sin hache. 'La otra noche bajamos a comer langosta.'* Mmmmm. Can I have some? *¿Uds. comieron langosta?"* | ("'The other…' without h, is without an h. 'The other night we went down to eat lobster.') Mmmmm. Can I have some? (You guys ate lobster?") |

After reading two or three more sentences, Matilde comments, "That's nice, very good job."

Capital letters and punctuation also get their turn along with the praise.

*"La ge otra vez, minúscula, no se hace mayúscula. ¿Qué pasa al final de la oración? Punto. Tú estás haciendo muy bien, en escribir. Estoy muy contenta, pero..."*

("The *g* again, small letter, we don't use the capital. What happens at the end of the sentence? Period. You're doing very well in writing. I'm very happy, but...")

Grammar can also mitigate the praise. "You did a good job, only you have a couple of things with the grammar. *'¿A mí me gustas?'* ('I likes it?')"

Most of Matilde's praise is reserved for art work. The comment "Very nice" is much more likely to be directed at drawing than at writing. An Eskimo print elicits "Hey, that came out nice." A coloring book page of an Aztec calendar is shown to the whole class with the pronouncement, "This is very nice, the way that Camilo has colored it in."

The greatest praise and excitement about the children's work occurs when they have done a good job on the art work for a **big book** created by the class. Class-constructed big books occupy a place of importance in Matilde's classroom. Teacher and students may spend days thinking about what they're going to write. The text is jointly constructed, sometimes as a variation on a book that Matilde has read to them several times, sometimes as a compilation of what they have learned, or what they want to say about a certain topic. For one of the big books they write this year, they use the pattern from a book called *If You Give a Mouse a Cookie*. This is a cumulative cause-and-effect story in which each action causes a reaction; eventually the story comes back to where it started, giving a mouse a cookie. The children have decided to write their adaptation about one of the girls in the class; their big book is entitled *If You Give Diara a Flower*. They have already decided on the first two lines, and Matilde writes them on the board: "If you give Diara a flower, she will sneeze. Then she will want a tissue to clean her nose. When you give her the tissue, she'll probably ask..." "Now," says Matilde, "we have to continue from here. It has to be consensus." One child suggests something directly from *If You Give a Mouse a Cookie*. Matilde's comment is, "We don't want to use things from here. We want to adapt, we don't want to plagiarize." Somebody suggests that Diara might want to take a bath. Matilde erases "ask" and makes the sentence on the board say, "When you give her the tissue, she'll probably want to take a bath." The children talk about wanting a towel after she takes a bath. Matilde writes, "After the bath she would ask for a towel." A child suggests something about a flower. Matilde responds, "We're doing this in sequence. She already has a flower." Of course, at the end of the book they do come back to the flower, but not before the students decide that Diara should change her clothes, brush her hair, ask for a kiss, go to the mall (it was decided by class vote that she should go to the mall rather than going to the park, playing, drawing, or sleeping), go to Burger King (it took another vote to decide whether it should be Burger King or McDonald's), meet some friends, go to the park, and see a beautiful flower, and, finally, that one of her friends should give Diara a flower.

**Investigations**

Discuss with a colleague how Matilde's interactions with her students reflect her expectations of them.

If you give Diara a flower,
she will sneeze.

Over the next few days Matilde copies the text of the story onto large pieces of oaktag, one sentence per page. The children work in pairs illustrating each page. There is a lot of direction from Matilde, reminders to plan what they are going to draw before they do it, to make their illustrations large enough to fill the whole page, to use a variety of materials, to be realistic, to use the special "Color My Friends" crayons to get authentic skin colors. When all the pages are done and ready to be bound, Matilde shows them to the class. "I love this one here of Diara and the flower. She's sneezing and the petals are blowing all over the place. They did a very good job on here. She used different kinds of mediums, she used the construction paper to make the flowers. Use what we have in this classroom. Use different kinds of things to make the pictures look better. I think you guys did a very good thing here. Mariana, I like this bathtub, the shower, and the water's flowing out of the *ducha* (shower) here. She asks to take a bath, and so she goes to take a bath. I want you guys to practice your drawing skills at all times. Remember when you go shopping with your parents, instead of asking for toys, ask for crayons and coloring pencils. Practice at home and your skills will get better. This one here is one of my favorite pages. When she looked in the mirror, what happened to her hair? She started to have a bad hair day. She goes 'Aaaaaccccchhhhhh' when she sees her hair standing on end there. And she has on *chancletas* (sandals), they did a good job there. This has some nice detail, someone decided to put a TV in the room. You can't be without your entertainment, right?"

This kind of teasing affection is typical of Matilde's interactions with the children. Her teasing takes many different forms:

| | |
|---|---|
| "*Ángela quiere vender sus varicelas; ¿quién quiere comprarlas?*" | ("Ángela wants to sell her chicken pox; who wants to buy them?") |

When she asks Omar to clean up the mess under his desk, she says, "Omar, you want to take the broom and sweep up under your desk. It looks like you're building a nest there." Half an hour later, Omar is still sweeping, and Matilde laughingly comments, "If you give Omar a broom, he'll want to sweep the whole room. And he'll sweep, and he'll sweep, and he'll sweep."

Matilde's affection for the children is obvious in other ways. The first few minutes of every Monday morning are spent talking with the children about what they did over the weekend, and she reminds them that they shouldn't watch too much TV or play in dangerous places. She comments whenever she has seen a child outside of school ("Guess who I-I-I-I saw last night,") and compliments the children on new hairdos or new clothes. Sometimes this is just "Your hair looks nice," spoken to Nina when she comes in with her hair in a pony tail instead of her usual long braid. At other times Matilde teases: "Hey, Inés, you've got paw prints all over your shirt; what happened, did a dog walk all over your shirt?"

Matilde believes that it's important to show affection. When a child mentions that she doesn't give *abrazos* (hugs) to her brother on Valentine's Day, Matilde talks about how important it is to show affection; hugs are more important than candy.

**Investigations**

List the things that are important in Matilde's classroom. What would you add or delete from this list for your own classroom?

> *"Abrazos valen más; la gente necesita abrazos. Yo doy abrazos a Uds. aquí."*
>
> ("Hugs are worth more; people need hugs. I give you guys hugs here.")

The children feel secure and comfortable in her classroom. When she has to reprimand them, it is with the sense that she is doing it for their own good. Reprimands are sometimes necessary in response to poor behavior in the cafeteria or on the playground, but in the classroom the children very seldom need to be reprimanded for anything they do. Matilde sets very high expectations for behavior in her room, and the children live up to those expectations. Fights do not occur; courtesy reigns. The most she might have to do is remind a child that he or she should be working instead of talking or daydreaming.

*Observe a teacher who claims to be using a whole language approach and compare what you observe with what you have read about in Matilde's classroom. Give possible reasons for similarities and differences you find.*

**Investigations**

Observation

———————

The implementation of these varied activities looks effortless. One day Matilde gets up from her desk, goes to a bin of books on the bookshelf by the door, flips through the books until she finds the one she wants, and reads it to the children. That's how the Native American unit began. Before the unit was finished, the children completed several major art projects and consulted innumerable reference books. They used Native American pictographs to write about themselves, and learned and performed a Native American chant. Simply collecting the materials needed for all these activities involves an immense amount of time, and yet the impression given is that Matilde just goes to the right spot in the room, gets what she wants, and uses it.

Of course it's not that easy. The Native American unit is a new one this year.

**Frameworks**

Involvement, pp. 86-89.

**Investigations**

List all the ways you can think of that teachers decide what topics they are going to use for units.

How does Matilde decide what to do and how to do it? *"Well, what I do is decide on some of the things that interest me, and sometimes I ask the kids what they would like to do. The Native American unit was something I was interested in doing, because the Native American Indians wanted to make a casino here in Massachusetts.*

*"Once we decide on the unit we're going to do, I usually go to the library and see what books they have, or what information they have, and try to get information that I can give to them at their levels, that they will be able to understand. I also try to find units that are done and maybe they have some activities that I haven't planned for. I bought a unit on Native Americans, but it came a little late, and some of the things that were in there, I said, 'We're doing this; we did that.'*

*"Like the buckskins that we did with them, that was part of teaching the children about some of the things that the Native Americans did with the animals, explaining to them that all parts of the animals were used for everything. So we also tried to find pictures that depicted them using the different parts of the animal, how they dried them out and everything, so those little pieces of paper were more or less how they dried out the skin of the animal. Making the Indian village that we did, that was based on different homes that they used. We had books on Native American homes, and clothing and everything, and we also had all kinds of little pictures that depict different things about the American Indians. Doing these units can be exciting, but they require a lot of work, just deciding, and researching. Because you try to do a bibliography, the books that you need to refer to, just teacher resource books, and then the bibliography for the children."*

At the same time that she was explaining about how much work it had been to put this unit together, Matilde was already planning in her head how she would adapt the unit when she taught it again the following year: *"It was exciting, and I think next year I'm going to do it too, but a little differently than what we did this year. I think next year we'll do a **big book** on Native Americans, so the children can discuss what they learned. It'll be a book that they can read, and it's going to be fun. I like doing that. One thing I wanted to do was bring in a Native American speaker, but at the Native American Council, they wanted a fee, and I decided we couldn't afford a fee. But then I met a parent, and she's Native American, and I told her that next year when we do our unit I'm going to have her come in and speak to the children. We see these pictures of Native American Indians here, but they're the same as you and me, they put on the same clothes and everything. It was amazing the questions that were generated by these children, what they thought about Native Americans. So it's always interesting, and it's fun."*

**Investigations**

Observation

*Think about your own planning processes, or interview another teacher about his or hers. Compare these processes with Matilde's. If there are differences or similarities, give possible reasons for them.*

_____

Matilde also thinks that working with computers is fun. She would like to have more of them so she could use them across the curriculum. *"For me, I'm glad, I'm thrilled. I can see so many things that I can do with the computer with the children. I don't want to rely all the time on the computer, but I do want to see them become computer literate, so they can do different things on it, not just see it as, 'Oh, we're going to play a game.' No, I want them to use it as an instrument of learning."*

The computers in Room 7 are used mainly as a tool by the children when they write their daily journals. Over the buzz of purposeful talk, Matilde's voice can occasionally be heard announcing, "The Bank Street Writer is available." This is a reminder to the eight or ten children who write their journals on the computer that they should not forget to do so. The children watch to see when the computer is free, then go over and sit down, write three or four sentences, and print out what they have written. They erase whatever's on the screen when they finish, without saving their work. They take the printout back to their seats and draw pictures to illustrate what they have written, usually spending more time drawing the pictures than they did writing the journal. When they finish, they put this new journal page into a file folder with their previous entries.

The children who use the computers to write their journals are the more advanced writers in the class. Matilde had mentioned to some of the other children that she would teach them to use the computer so they could write their journals on it, too, but she didn't find the time to do that, and they continued writing their journals by hand.

In addition to the Bank Street Writer, there are two other computers in the classroom. The children use them when they have indoor recess, usually to practice basic addition and subtraction facts up to ten with the *Math Rabbit* program. Matilde said that the children used the computers more in the beginning of the year, but that she had to sit with them too much because the programs are in English and the children couldn't remember what the commands were.

The modem that is connected to the Apple IIe sits unused. In previous years it had been used for penpal exchanges with the fifth-grade students in the same school, and also with another school across town. Then the communications software went on the blink, the school system changed the telephones, and Matilde had trouble getting back into the local network. She has signed up for a program that will give her access to the **Internet** next year, although she's not yet sure exactly what she's going to do with the telecommunications capability. *"I would like to do something in terms of making connections with children, maybe in South America. When we went for our interview, Chuck, who's going to be our mentor, connected us to a bulletin board that was from South America, and there were all kinds of people looking to establish a relationship with people to converse in Spanish and to do little projects."* It becomes apparent that Matilde is aware of the potential of telecommunications when she says, *"Hey, we can maybe connect to Syracuse and go into their information system, maybe find some author. For instance, let's look and see what they have on Tomie de Paolo, what information they have on him."*

The children also get a chance to use computers in the computer classroom, where they go twice a week for instruction on IBM Jr. PCs. What they do in the computer room has little connection with what they're doing in the classroom. Some days they work on programs that drill math facts; other days it's *Reader*

Frameworks

Technology, pp. 90-93.

Investigations

List other ways in which telecommunications could be used in a bilingual classroom.

List advantages and disadvantages of using drill programs such as *Math Rabbit* and *Reader Rabbit*.

*Rabbit* who drills them on phonics facts. When Ms. Marcus, the computer teacher, introduces a new drawing program, she explains what she wants them to do before they begin: "Today we're going to do something new. You have to pay attention—if you don't, you'll be lost. If you want to write a story, you can pick the picture that goes with your story and put it on the screen. It will be best if you write your story on a paper. Here's a list of all the pictures there are on the computer. You pick all your pictures and you put them on the screen. Then when you pick all the pictures that you want, you can write your story. When you're done, I'll print it out. Here's one that I did. See the pictures? You can't see the colors, but when you see it on the screen, you'll see the colors. Let me show you how you're going to do it. Whenever you want to write a story, you print the letter *M* on your keyboard. If you don't like the background you get, you print the letter *S*. Keep on pressing the letter *S* until you find one that you like. Now what are we going to do to put the pictures in it? Press the letter *F*. Do you want this boy in your picture? No? Try another one. Keep pressing the letter *F* until you find the picture you want. To go back, press *B* for back. How do we put the picture in the screen? Press the *P*. *P* means 'pick' this object. To move the picture, press the arrow key. Once you get all the pictures you want, then you start writing your story. But today I don't want you to write. I just want you to get familiar with all the pictures. Take a computer, get familiar with the keys."

A few of the children may have understood the directions well enough to create a picture on the computer screen immediately. Most of them, however, figure it out by trial and error. A few simply wait for Ms. Marcus to come and show them individually what to do. They spend the next half hour pasting pictures into different backgrounds, erasing them, and doing it again.

The children also spend a couple of months in the computer room working with a program designed to teach touch typing skills. Only a few of them have the patience to use the correct fingers when they are practicing. Some of the girls apparently understand that if they practice diligently they will learn to type easily. (Watching the observer in their classroom taking field notes on a portable computer was an inspiration to many of them.) Few of the boys, however, seem to grasp the concept of delayed reward; they are willing to do whatever the screen tells them to do—tasks such as copying *asa, sas, asa*—but they are not willing to think about which fingers they should be using.

Observation

*Observe students using computers in various ways and compare the uses with those in Matilde's classroom and in the computer room of her school. What factors might account for similarities and differences you observe?*

---

Language Use, pp. 94-100.

When asked if she has any rationale or principles governing her choice of which language to use at any particular time, Matilde replies, "No, *it's automatic. We speak Spanish. This year we did a lot more speaking in English than we've ever done, and I was glad, because I thought the children needed that. We actually implemented a little more ESL, since the children take computers in English, and they have Mr. Goodwin, the science teacher, in English. That completed our ESL portion; we didn't really need to do any other ESL."*

Spanish is taken for granted in the classroom, just as it is in Matilde's mind. Everybody understands Spanish, but not everybody understands English, so anything of importance is done in Spanish. This includes lectures on behavior, explanations of important notices that are being sent home, instructions for projects that have to look good. Reading is done in Spanish, and the children do all their writing in Spanish. The only English that slips into their writing consists of things like the names of movies or television shows, or direct quotes of something that was said in English. Some of the children's oral communication is almost entirely in English, and there are very few reminders to use Spanish. Only when discussing phonics-related elements such as beginning letters or rhyming words does Matilde remind them to use Spanish. When she asks, *"Bicicleta, ¿con qué empieza?"* ("Bicycle, what does it begin with?") and a student answers "bee" in English, her response is, *"No, estamos hablando en español, es la be."* ("No, we're speaking Spanish, it's *be*.") Searching for the word *red* (net) in Spanish to rhyme with *usted* (you), she asks,

Guess what approximate percentage of each language Matilde uses. Compare your guess with your colleagues'.

| | |
|---|---|
| *"¿Cómo se llama esa cosa que usamos para pescar? Nosotros lo hemos usado aquí para el acuario."* | ("What's the name of that thing that we use to fish? We've used it here for the aquarium.") |

When Marisol answers "nest," Matilde ignores the confusion between English words and reminds her that *"Estamos buscando en español."* ("We're looking in Spanish.")

Outside of a few incidents such as these, there is no control over which language is used. Two children, Julio and Marisol, seem to prefer to use English most of the time. Several others, Ignacio, Iris, Lucy, Mariana, Evita, Inés, Omar, and Nicolás, among them, are comfortable using either or both languages, and do so as the situation demands. There are others who obviously have more difficulty in English—Nina, Fernando, Dorita—and use it only when they have to. Yoni and Ángela are just learning English, but use whatever they know whenever they can, and Jorge is increasing his comprehension daily but seems to avoid speaking English.

Matilde's use of the two languages makes a fascinating study in **codeswitching.** She grew up in a Puerto Rican family in New York and has always lived in communities in which both English and Spanish are used, separately and together. Because all her schooling was in English, Matilde considers that to be her stronger language, but her Spanish is totally fluent, if not always correct according to "standard" Spanish. Her code switches are fluent, grammatical, and usually motivated by something in the situational or linguistic context. It may be the person she is talking to, the language used by that person, the thing she is talking about, the desire to ensure that everybody understands, or a borrowed word that triggers a switch. For example, a change from talking to the entire class to talking to a single student can cause a switch. During dictation, which is always in Spanish, she switches to English when she addresses Camilo individually:

| | |
|---|---|
| *"Hagan un triángulo violeto en su papel. Al lado del once."* | ("Make a purple triangle on your paper. Next to the eleven.) |

Do you have purple? You can borrow a purple from your neighbor."

A response in the other language will often cause Matilde to switch languages, perhaps without even realizing it. When talking about maple syrup as part of the Native American unit, Matilde begins in English because she is going to read the students a book about maple syrup in English. She asks, "Do you remember what we said yesterday about maple syrup? Yes, Fernando." Fernando answers, *"Lo sacan de los árboles,"* ("They get it from the trees,") and Matilde continues the lesson in Spanish:

| | |
|---|---|
| *"Sí, jarabe de los árboles. Y, ¿quiénes lo sacan? Al principio, ¿quiénes empezaron a sacar el jarabe de los árboles? Los indios, y ellos enseñaron a los blancos a sacar el jarabe de los árboles."* | ("Yes, syrup from the trees. And who gets it? At the beginning, who started to get the syrup from the trees? The Indians, and they taught the white men to get the syrup from the trees.") |

Sometimes Matilde says something to the whole class in English and then repeats it in Spanish to ensure that everyone understands. When she wants to find out if all the children have listened to a taped book as part of the Native American unit, Matilde asks, "Who has not listened to the 'Legend of the Indian Paint Brush?' *¿Quién no ha escuchado esa historia?"* (Who hasn't listened to that story?") This kind of immediate translation does not happen very often, however.

Some of Matilde's switches have the effect of emphasizing what she is saying. This occurs most often when she has to reprimand a child who speaks both languages well. Julio often has to be reminded what he's supposed to be doing: "Can I see your paper?"

| | |
|---|---|
| *¿Tienes nombre aquí? ¿Qué te dije que hicieras? ¿Por qué tú estabas allí? ¿Por qué?* | (Do you have your name here? What did I tell you to do? Why were you there? Why?) |

I want to know, why were you there? Who asked you to get up and go over there?"

Discourse Analysis, p. 118.

Quotations will often cause a code switch to maintain the same language in which they were originally spoken. Once she has switched so as to repeat the quote, Matilde often continues in the language she switched into. Here she is reminding the children to include the punctuation when they copy a **language experience** story from the blackboard: *"Allí, las cosas que yo tengo nombradas* ("There, the things that I named,) 'went to the park, the mall,' put in the commas, please. Where the commas are, don't forget the punctuation."

Because Spanish is taken for granted in Matilde's classroom there is no celebration of children's achievements in that language. There is, however, a subtle celebration of learning English. Favorable comments are made when the newest arrivals say something in English. As the year goes on, more and more English is addressed directly to these children, and they begin to use whatever English they know whenever they can. In a few short weeks, Yoni progresses from "Q-ee" for "Excuse me" through "Q me" to "Quze me," and he uses that and "Move" with everybody, including his Spanish-speaking classmates. His English responses become more and more frequent as the year progresses, and he can often be heard repeating English phrases that others have used: "Sit down, sit, sit, sit down," "Everybody, everybody, everybody," "Oh-five-one" (his bus number). When Matilde comments to the class that "It's co-o-o-o-ld outside," Yoni rejoins, "No, it's hot." When he doesn't understand what's going on in the classroom, however, he stops paying attention and begins to fool around with pencils, papers, or other children. On the other hand, when Ángela doesn't understand what's going on, she pretends she does, raising her hand constantly and contributing things that more often than not don't make any sense. She has picked up phrases such as "Wow, very good," "Oh, my goodness," "Look at this," and "Thank you very much," and uses them in more or less appropriate contexts. Ángela's interest in learning English is preserved for posterity when the class composes a **big book** about her. The children suggest the sentences that become the text of the big book: "The Little Old Lady doesn't want to speak Spanish now, she only wants to speak in English. She is trying to write in English. She speaks a little English."

Investigations

Discuss with a colleague reasons why Yoni and Ángela seem to be so anxious to learn English.

Some of the children receive formal ESL instruction. Nic-

olás, Freddie, Ignacio, Nina, and Diara are pulled out of the classroom for an hour with the ESL teacher each morning. When asked how it was determined which children would go to ESL, Matilde replies that these are the children who had begun English reading with the ESL teacher last year, so they continued with ESL this year. The two children who seem to prefer using English rather than Spanish, Julio and Marisol, are not among those who receive ESL instruction. One of the two children who tested "competent" in English on a **standardized test** of English reading and writing also does not receive ESL instruction.

The rest of the children get their "ESL instruction" through science and computer classes taught in English. In the computer class, Ms. Marcus talks so fast that she is difficult to understand. The children may learn some written English from the programs themselves, however. In science class, Mr. Goodwin will often ask another student to translate for those who don't understand something, rather than simplifying the language he uses and allowing the context of the student activity to provide the meaning. None of these teachers—Matilde, Ms. Marcus, and Mr. Goodwin—has any training in second language teaching techniques.

Observation

*Observe a bilingual teacher and note how he or she uses two languages, including how much each language is used; note examples of codeswitching. Compare what you observe with Matilde's language use and suggest reasons for similarities or differences.*

Assessment,
pp. 101–106.

There is no formal evaluation of students' English learning until the end of the year, when Matilde has to give all her students standardized tests of English proficiency. She says she hates the end of the year because of "all this stuff for ESL." She administers the *IDEA Oral Language Proficiency Test*, an individual test of listening and speaking ability, and the *Language Assessment Scales, Reading and Writing (LAS R/W)*, a group test of English reading and writing ability, plus fills out all the forms needed for reporting the test results and recommending placements for next year.

In responding to the questions on the *IDEA* test, the children can't help trying to turn the questions into meaningful conversational exchanges. When Matilde asks Camilo, "Do you drive your father's car?" the expected answer is "No, I don't drive my father's car." Camilo replies, "No, I ride," and Matilde responds "The question isn't about ride; it's about drive. Do you drive your father's car? Give me a sentence with *drive*." Matilde herself struggles against the lack of meaning in much of what she has to ask the children. When she asks Ignacio the question about driving his father's car, it becomes "Do you drive your father's truck?" In another part of the test, several of the questions involve decontextualized picture identification. The teacher is instructed to say, "What is this? This is a _____." Matilde can't help remarking "I know it looks a little odd there." She struggles in trying to elicit a complete sentence: "When I say 'What is this?' you say 'This is a pencil.' What is this? I want you to say a full sentence. What? I want a whole sentence. I asked you 'What is this?' and you say 'This is a pencil.' What is this?" The commands she has to give must seem as senseless to her as they do to the children: "Put the pencil under the table." She laughs when Jorge simply repeats the command. "Please stand up and turn around." (The "please" was added spontaneously; the written instructions from which Matilde is reading do not include it.) She sounds a little impatient as she says to Ignacio, "What are you supposed to do? Did you turn around? You have to do everything I ask you to do."

Discuss with a colleague all the reasons you can think of why Matilde was surprised her students did so well on this test.

Matilde does not expect the children to do well on the writing portion of the LAS R/W test: *"You know, they write phonetically, so they wouldn't get the score."* She seems surprised as she corrects their tests and discovers sentence completions that are correct. "This one here, that's fine: '(We are going shopping and then) going home.' (Parentheses indicate the portion of the sentence that was given on the test.) That's spelled right. This one here he would get: '(My mom was tired because) she came from work.'" Talking about the test later, she discusses how well the children did. *"I was very surprised, the kids did quite well. I didn't think they would do well on it. It was amazing, I actually let them do it, you know, and they went through it, and we had two that came out competent, literate. That was Diara, which was a very good surprise, and Lucy. Next year they'll be mainstreamed for English reading because they scored so well."*

This year Matilde's students don't have to take the Spanish **criterion-referenced tests** (CRTs) that are normally given at the end of the academic year. Matilde is disappointed. *"What I really like at the end of the year is when we do the CRT, that really gives me an idea whether they've learned the skills that they need to know for that grade level. This year we didn't give it, for some reason it was not given to us this year, I don't know why. I was looking forward to giving it because we go through and we correct it, and it really lets me know what skills they need to work on more."*

Because these students are in a second-grade bilingual classroom, they do not have to take the **standardized achievement tests** that are given to students in monolingual classrooms. Students who have been in bilingual classes three years or more must take the achievement tests, and teachers of other bilingual students are encouraged to give them for practice. Matilde's comment about that was, *"They've been in a bilingual program since kindergarten, so they can't read this. I'd have to read it to them."*

Although Matilde's students don't have to take the achievement tests, she is concerned that test scores in the school are going down. *"The scores have gone down, very, very low. That was one of my contentions this year, that maybe something should be done for the upper grades, third, fourth and fifth, that they really need to tighten a little bit more how they teach the curriculum objectives and not utilize so much **whole language** for those kids, because I think they really need to be taught how to take a test, and the basics of those tests. I'm being told, 'We don't rely on the standardized tests,' but that's what the school department looks at, how high those scores are, how low they are, and how they continue to be lowered. So they're going to order some kind of system that will be distributed to these teachers so they can deal with teaching the children how to take tests, so they can do a better showing on the achievement tests."*

Even without achievement tests, the children in Room 7 get a lot of practice taking tests. There are practice spelling tests and final spelling tests every week. There are diagnostic dictations every month or so. There are occasional reading or math tests to tell the teacher how the children are doing. The children are used to taking tests.

The weekly lists of spelling words are taken from books the children are reading or have read, which could be anything from a trade book like *Corduroy* to the stories in the **basal readers**. Each week a new set of spelling word flash cards appears on the chalk tray in the front of the room. At designated times a different child will lead the class in reviewing the words by reading them from the flash cards, creating sentences using them, and clapping out the number of syllables in each word. Most of the children get very good grades on their spelling tests but consistently misspell the same words in their journals.

Spelling tests—*dictados*, they are called—are routinized. Yellow paper means it's a practice test. The teacher reads the words, repeating each word twice. Sometimes she gives little hints as in this example, where she reminds them about silent 'h' and about writing an 's' that they don't pronounce:

Discuss with a colleague what you think of Matilde's suggestions for raising test scores. What suggestions would you have?

| | |
|---|---|
| *"Número uno, hermano.* | ("Number one, *hermano*. What |
| *¿Cuál es la letra que no suena en* | letter has no sound in Spanish? |

| | |
|---|---|
| *español? Número dos, gusta.* | Number two, *gusta. Gussssta.* |
| *Gussssta. No quiero ver la* | I don't want to see the word |
| *palabra 'guta.' La palabra es* | *'guta.'* The word is *'gusta.'*" |
| *'gusta.' Número tres, sol. Sollll."* | Number three, *sol. Sollll."*) |

After the words are dictated (ten words for the advanced group, six words for the slower group), children are called on at random to read them back. The other children are expected to check their spelling as each word is read back. The good practice tests, the ones with 80, 90, or 100 percent correct, are displayed on the "Good Work" bulletin board.

The real spelling test follows exactly the same routine, but the words are written in small blue notebooks instead of on yellow paper, and fewer hints are given. The grades from the real test go into the teacher's rank book instead of on the bulletin board.

About once a month there is a special diagnostic *dictado*, including short phrases and sentences (capital letters and periods must be included), following directions (an important skill in this classroom), and math problems. Students who don't follow directions and try to complete a math problem as soon as it is dictated usually miss the next item, thus losing points; following directions is indeed important.

| | |
|---|---|
| *"OK, como siempre, Uds. con* | ("OK, as always with dicta- |
| *los dictados tienen que prestar* | tions, you have to pay attention. |
| *atención. No preguntas.* | No questions.) |

No one is talking. *Sumen cinco más cinco más siete.* (Add five plus five plus seven.) I do not want to see you erasing; if you make a mistake, X it out and continue. *Número dos. Escriban 'plato.' Tres. Dibujen un ojo.* (Number two. Write 'plate.' Three. Draw an eye.) Dorita, looking at your paper.

| | |
|---|---|
| *Cuatro. Resten quinientos* | (Four. Subtract five hundred |
| *cuarenta y dos… quinientos* | forty-two… five hundred |
| *cuarenta y dos menos* | forty-two minus four hundred |
| *cuatrocientos uno.* | one.) |

Camilo, you look at your paper.

| | |
|---|---|
| *Número cuatro, restar,* | (Number four, subtraction,) |
| take-away, *quinientos cuarenta y* | take-away, (five hundred forty- |
| *dos menos cuatrocientos uno.* | two minus four hundred one.) |

You may not have time to do the whole computation right now. When I finish all twelve items you may go back and begin the different processes. *Cinco. Escriban 'zapato.' Escriban 'zapato.'* (Five. Write 'shoe.' Write 'shoe.'

| | |
|---|---|
| *Seis. Escriban la palabra 'camión.'* | Six. Write the word 'truck.' This |
| *Esta parte, número seis, tiene* | part, number six, has two parts. |
| *dos partes. Parte A, escriban la* | Part A, write the word 'truck.' |
| *palabra 'camión.' Parte B es rimar* | Part B is to rhyme a word with |
| *una palabra con 'camión.'* | 'truck.' Write a word that |

*Escriban una palabra que rime con 'camión.' No me digan nada. Dije escriban.*

rhymes with 'truck.' Don't say anything. I said write.)

You're not talking to me. When I'm talking to you guys you don't respond to me. You respond on your paper.

*OK, número siete. Completen esta oración. 'Mi casa es blanco.' No tienen que escribir la oración. Yo dije completen la oración con ~~una palabra. Escriban una palabra~~ para llenar la oración. Comprendan lo que yo quiero. Completen la oración 'Mi casa es... blanco.' Llenen el espacio. ¿Mi casa es qué?*

(OK, number seven. Complete this sentence. 'My house is blank.' You don't have to write the sentence. I said complete the sentence with a word. Write one word to fill in the sentence. Understand what I want. Complete the sentence 'My house is... blank.' Fill in the space. My house is what?

*Ocho. Sumen. Veintitrés, once, más treinta y cuatro. Sumen veintitrés, once, y treinta y cuatro. Sumen.*

Eight. Add. Twenty-three, eleven, plus thirty-four. Add twenty-three, eleven, and thirty-four. Add.

*Nueve. Escriban 'papel.'*

Nine. Write 'paper.'

*Número diez. Quitar. Van a restar. Trescientos veinticinco quiten diecinueve. No hay tiempo para resolver el problema, pero Uds. van a regresar después cuando yo termine. Número diez. Quitar; trescientos veinticinco resten diecinueve.*

Number ten. Take-away. You're going to subtract. Three hundred twenty-five take away nineteen. There isn't time to solve the problem, but you're going to come back afterwards when I finish. Number ten. Take away; three hundred twenty-five minus nineteen.

Compare the objectives implicit in this *dictado* with the objectives implicit in Matilde's teaching of language arts and mathematics as described on pp. 20-33.

*Once. Escriban la oración que yo dicto. ¿Están listos para once? 'Los niños están afuera.' Número once. 'Los niños están afuera.'*

Eleven. Write the sentence that I dictate. Are you ready for eleven? 'The boys are outside.' Number eleven. 'The boys are outside.'

*Doce. Escriban dos palabras que comiencen con la letra ese. Doce. Escriban dos palabras que comiencen con la letra ese."*

Twelve. Write two words that begin with the letter *s*. Twelve. Write two words that begin with the letter *s*.")

Usually dictations are corrected later and given back to the students the next day, but this time Matilde corrects them immediately and calls students to her desk for feedback as she does so. "Teresa, come over here.

| | |
|---|---|
| *Camión, camión, no. Tiene que ser una palabra que rime. Camión, ladrón. Camión, listón. Camión, buzón."* | (Truck, truck, no. It has to be a word that rhymes. Truck, luck. Truck, duck. Truck, buck." ) |
| *"Jorge, ¿tú no sabes lo que son palabras que riman? ¿No estudiamos ese concepto? ¿Cuál es una palabra que rima con 'camión'? Estoy esperando, Jorge. ¿No me puedes decir? Entonces no aprendiste palabras que riman. ¿Quién puede dar a ese caballero una palabra que rime con 'camión'?"* | ("Jorge, you don't know what rhyming words are? Didn't we study that concept? What's a word that rhymes with 'truck'? I'm waiting, Jorge. You can't tell me? Then you didn't learn rhyming words. Who can give this gentlemen a word that rhymes with 'truck'?") |

"Who is Little Bird? (Several of the students consistently label their papers with the names they chose for themselves as part of the Native American unit.)

| | |
|---|---|
| *Siempre te olvidas de la puntuación, ¿verdad? Yo dije que escribieras la oración completa. ¿Está dónde? ¿Termina con qué?* | ("You always forget the punctuation, right? I said that you should write a complete sentence. It's where? What does it end with?) |

I want to see capital letters. You didn't do bad on here, but remember the punctuation. I'm going to wear a costume that says 'Punctuation' on it."
"Fernando, can I see you please?

| | |
|---|---|
| *'Camión, cayó'. ¿Cómo que 'cayó' rima con 'camión'? Yo les dije a Uds. más de dos veces. La palabra tiene que rimar con 'camión.' 'Mi casa es bonita.' Yo dije escribir una palabra para completar la oración. Yo no dije escribir la oración.* | ('Truck, tree.' How does 'tree' rhyme with 'truck'? I told you guys more than two times. The word has to rhyme with 'truck.' 'My house is pretty.' I said to write a word to complete the sentence. I didn't say to write the sentence.) |

What does this word mean? What's this word here? *Eso no es 'seis.' 'Seis' es así.* (That isn't 'six'; 'six' is like this.) I'm looking for your correct spelling on the word. You know how to spell 'six.' One, two, three, four, five. That's not high, Fernando. I need you to pay more attention, please."
"Nicolás, can I see you please? Yicky, what a dirty paper! Yuck! What kind of pencil are you using? A dirty pencil? Look at that, yuck! Three hundred twenty-five. You have to regroup, right? What does this word mean? One, two, three; three wrong."

To the whole class, Matilde announces, "You know what you guys made most of your mistakes at? In the math part. OK, three hundred twenty-five

> *quita diecinueve. Si el puesto no*    (minus nineteen. If the place
> *lleva ningún número, Uds. saben*    doesn't have any number, you
> *que es cero.*    know it's zero.)

And you forgot to do regrouping. And the sentence. You left the *s* off of 'boys.' And you didn't put *punto* (period)."

There are other tests given occasionally. The teacher wants to know how the children are doing, or she just wants to give them practice taking tests. One day it is a Spanish reading test. The directions tell the children to read the sentence, look at the four pictures, and mark the picture that goes with the sentence. The first sentences are easy: *El niño corre. Este es mi papá.* (The boy is running. This is my dad.) They get progressively harder. By the time the children finish the 40 items in the comprehension section of the test they have to read short paragraphs and identify the picture that corresponds to the paragraph. Many of the pictures are not at all clear. The children might be able to understand the paragraph but still misinterpret the picture. This could also happen on the vocabulary section of the test, where they read a single word and mark which of four pictures corresponds to the word.

It becomes obvious that the children are misinterpreting the pictures when, on the second day they have been working on the test, Matilde goes to the blackboard and calls for their attention. She draws a picture on the board, tells the children that this is *un ala* (a wing), and explains that sometimes it is hard to tell what the pictures are, so they should read the words carefully. The picture she draws looks no more like a wing than does the one on the test.

For several of the students in the class this reading comprehension test becomes a listening comprehension test, as the teacher reads all of the items out loud to them.

> *"Aquí hay cuatro libros escolares.*    ("There are four textbooks
> *Busca los tres libros que están*    here. Look for the three books
> *cerrados. Luego marca de estos*    that are closed. Then mark,
> *cuatro libros el que está abierto."*    from these four books, the one
>    that is open.")

Matilde seems to want the children to do well on their tests. A great deal of help is given, even if these are just practice tests. During a diagnostic math test she circulates among them, helping individual students, while at the same time continually reminding them not to look at each other's papers and do their own work.

*Observe both formal and informal assessment activities in a bilingual classroom. What differences and similarities do you find compared to the assessment that occurs in Matilde's classroom? How might you explain them ?*

Observation

Most of the visual material on the walls of Matilde's room is in Spanish: *La estación es primavera* (The season is spring) is posted over the calendar; *¿Cómo* *se escribe?* (How do you write it?) heads a display of tricky spelling words in Spanish; above the blackboard there is a quotation from José Martí: *Los niños son la esperanza del mundo...* (Children are the hope of the world...); a bulletin board exhibits *Correo importante* (Important Mail); *Los colores* (Colors) are displayed on balloons on the closet door; hanging chart holders display songs and poems in Spanish; the art center is labeled *Rincón de arte* (Art Corner). Under the flag there is a chart with the Spanish version of the Pledge of Allegiance.

English is also visible on the walls, but less so. The bulletin board where students' best work is displayed is labeled "Future Stars Today." On the wall above that bulletin board is a display of the five senses, with labels in both English and Spanish. Another bilingual wall display shows geometric shapes labeled in both languages, but a display of color words printed on different colored animals has labels only in English. Some of the poems and charts hanging in various places around the room are in English, but there are more in Spanish.

**Culture, pp. 107-111.**

In addition to language, the walls reflect various aspects of Hispanic culture. During May the seasonal bulletin board displays pictures and artifacts from Mexico with the caption *Viva Méjico!* [sic]. On the wall above that bulletin board is a display of large colored pictures of *Los indios taínos de Puerto Rico* (The Taino Indians of Puerto Rico). Another bulletin board shows a map of North and South America. The title is *Somos de...* (We Are From...); the children's countries of origin are listed, with a piece of yarn connecting the name of the country to the place on the map: Estados Unidos, México, Guatemala, El Salvador, Colombia, Venezuela, Ecuador, Costa Rica, Nicaragua, Honduras, Puerto Rico, Republica Dominicana. This year there are no students from Mexico or Nicaragua, but the names of those countries remain.

Other than the wall displays, there are few outward manifestations of Hispanic culture in Matilde's classroom. Toward the end of the school year, however, two cultural celebrations occur. One is a commemoration of *Cinco de mayo* (May fifth—Mexican Independence Day), initiated by the third grade bilingual teacher, whose students are studying Mexico. Matilde tells her children, "Next week we have a program that we're going to be doing with Mrs. Martínez in the third grade. We're going to talk about the program tomorrow. It's going to be a Mexican activity. How many of you have Mexican parents? *¿Cuántos de Uds. tienen padres mexicanos?*" It takes quite a bit of discussion to determine that Camilo has an aunt who married a Mexican, and that Rosita's father is from Mexico.

During the next several days the children bring in items from Mexico for display on the bulletin board, color pictures of the Aztec calendar, and listen to a Mexican legend. On the fifth of May, Matilde calls several children to her desk. "Lucy, can I have you up here please? Liana, can I see you for a second, honey? Evita. OK, we're going to be going to Mrs. Martínez's classroom, as you guys know.

| *Uds. van a hacer preguntas a la clase de Mrs. Martínez sobre lo que pasó en el día cinco de mayo en México."* | (You guys are going to ask Mrs. Martínez's class questions about what happened on the fifth of May in Mexico.") |

She gives each girl a strip of paper and asks her to read the question. *¿Qué* *pasaba en México en el mil ochocientos sesenta y dos?* (What was happening in Mexico in 1862?) *¿Qué querían hacer los franceses?* (What did the French want to do?) *¿Cuántos soldados franceses había?* (How many French soldiers were there?) Matilde's children read the questions without any idea what they signify. These are things the third-grade class has been studying, and Mrs. Martínez prepared the questions.

Matilde continues calling children to her desk in groups of three, giving them numbered sentence strips and having them read the questions on the strips. When twelve children have questions they line up in order and practice reading their questions, with reminders from Matilde: *"En voz alta porque estás preguntando a la clase. Otra vez."* ("In a loud voice because you're asking the class. Again.") "I can't hear you." *"Tienen que esperar que la persona conteste."* ("You have to wait for the person to answer.") *"Una pregunta, tienes que leerla así."* ("A question, you have to read it like this.") She repeats the question the child has just read, slowly and very clearly.

The children practice singing *Las mañanitas* and then go to the third-grade classroom, where the principal talks to them about Mexican history. Both classes show off what they have learned by asking and answering questions and singing songs. The celebration concludes with everybody enjoying tacos, chili, and a Mexican salad.

The other cultural observance occurs at the end of the school year, when the children dance a *plena*—a Puerto Rican folk dance—on their "graduation" day and the parents bring in foods typical of their native countries. Preparations begin about the middle of May. The boys are told that they will have to wear navy blue pants and short-sleeved white shirts. Matilde has dresses for the girls. Mariana asks whether they get to keep the dresses. "No, those are my dresses; they belong here. After graduation is over, you're going to give me the dresses back. The boys are going to use scarves, we have yellow scarves that you're going to put on, and we have *sombreros* too, and you're going to use *machetes*, because we're doing a folkloric dance. We want to be very typical *campesinos*, we want to be country persons for the occasion. We're going to have guests here for that day, and I want you to start talking with your parents already about graduation. We're going to ask that your parents bring in food, from each one of the countries.

| | |
|---|---|
| *Tienen que traer la comida y todo ese día para la celebración. Tienen que empezar a hablar a sus padres."* | (They have to bring the food and everything that day for the celebration. You have to start to talk to your parents.") |

A week later, the children are practicing the dance. *"Todos de pie. OK, pongan las manos en la cintura.* ("Everybody standing up. OK, put your hands on your waist.) OK, we're just going to move our hips, eh? Come on, Nina, liven up a little. Evita, move, like this. Your knees are moving, too. *Tienes que mover las rodillas también.* (You have to move your knees, too.) We're not doing any side stretches. Julio, we're not doing like this, we're going from side to side. Have a little problem there, Inés? Good, Diara. Keep it like that, move your hands back and forth. Nicolás, we're not going like this, *así no* (not like this). Come on, keep it moving. OK, sit down. You look good."

"Graduation" day arrives. The children are in their best party clothes and on their best behavior. The desks in the classroom are pushed together to make room for rows of chairs for the guests. The children read poems and stories. There are awards for conduct and attendance; Diara receives both of them. She also gets a reading award, as does Lucy. Liana receives the writing award, and Omar and Inés get mathematics awards. All the children are being promoted except Yoni and Ángela, who had not gone to school before this year, Dorita, who has been diagnosed with lead poisoning, and Fatima, who is a special education student.

Then the girls change out of their party dresses and into matching sundresses with a bright yellow, red, and orange print, with bows in their hair. The boys put on their yellow neckerchiefs and straw hats and pick up their cardboard *machetes*. They dance amazingly well for second graders. Following the dance, a mountain of food disappears—rice, more rice, rice and beans, rice and chicken, rice and pork, roast pork, more roast pork—with compliments to all the cooks.

In spite of there being few outward manifestations of Hispanic culture in Room 7, the culture is very much a part of everything that occurs there. Hispanic values are reflected in many different ways. One of the value systems that differs from many Anglo classrooms is the way time is used. Nobody pays any attention to the schedule. Everything that is not determined by the Anglo time system of the school as a whole is flexible. It doesn't matter what the schedule says; different subjects and activities may occur at any time of the day, or they may not occur at all. Transitions between one activity and another are seamless. Pacing might appear slow to an Anglo, but is obviously very comfortable for both teacher and students.

Another aspect of the use of time with which both teacher and students are comfortable is Matilde's ability to do many things at once. What to an observer might seem like interruptions are more likely manifestations of her polychronic nature. For example, one morning Matilde is sitting at the round table copying lists of spelling words onto ditto masters so she can duplicate them to send home as homework. While doing this she reminds the students who have just returned from ESL that they have to finish the work in their writing folders this week. "OK, the kids who came in now, are any of you waiting for a writing conference? I want all of your books finished this week. You have until Friday. Fernando, did you ask for a conference? Marisol, did you take your name off the conference sheet?" Still writing, she says to Yoni, *"Yoni, déjame ver tu reading folder, please."* ("Yoni, let me see your reading folder, please.") He brings her the pages from his writing folder. "Your reading folder, reading folder." He is unable to find what she wants. *"Yoni, el reading folder tuyo."* ("Yoni, the reading folder of yours.") He replies, *"No tengo,"* ("I don't have one,") still unsure of what she wants. *"Sí, que usamos cuando estás en el grupo."* ("Yes, that we use when you're in the group.") Finally understanding, he retrieves it from his desk as Matilde calls to Inés, who has taken a laminated math sheet out of the math center and is returning to her desk with it. "Inés, come here.

*Eso es tan sencillo, no quiero que cojas eso. Te dije muchas veces."*

(That's so simple, I don't want you to take that one. I told you that many times.")

In the meantime, Matilde has looked at Yoni's reading folder and given it back

**Investigations**

Discuss with a colleague what you think children learn from participating in cultural celebrations such as those described here.

to him, at the same time saying to Mariana, "What are you doing, Mariana?

| | |
|---|---|
| *¿Ya terminaste con el libro?* | (Did you already finish with the |
| *Entonces, ¿qué derecho tienes* | book? Then what right do you |
| *a estar allí sin hacer nada?"* | have to be there without |
| | doing anything?") |

All this time, she has been copying spelling words onto ditto sheets.

Family is another Hispanic value that is conspicuous in Matilde's classroom. She knows the parents of all the children, and most of their brothers and sisters as well. She knows and cares about their families, who is sick and who is well, who has new babies or new cars, who has relatives visiting or come to stay. She knows when they go to Puerto Rico for vacation, to New York for the weekend, or to Pepe's Diner for dinner. Both her family and the children's families are present in much of what happens in the classroom. Family provides the context for classroom activities and discussions, as Matilde shares her own childrens' activities, illnesses, and special events with her students, and they share with her.

Matilde maintains communication with the parents of all of the children in her classroom. She has a telephone in her room, and a question about behavior, missing homework, why a child is absent, or recovery from a tonsillectomy will result in an immediate telephone call. Parents stop into the classroom frequently, to talk about students' progress, drop off a child who missed the bus, bring a forgotten sweater, or just say hello. Mothers who can only get to school by coming on the school bus with their children are welcome to stay for the day, helping out in any way they like while they are there. Matilde complains about parental support, however. *"When the kids come to kindergarten, the parents are there. They want to know, they want to see what they can do to help the child. But midway through first grade, when they see that the kid's doing well, they don't continue to inquire. They say, 'Oh, well, he's doing well,' and especially after the report card comes out, they say, 'Oh, the kid is doing good, no problem.' But you still have to inquire about how that child is doing, to see what else you can help the child do to get better. So at first we get a lot of parental involvement in the school. Then it starts to lessen more and more as the kid goes up, into the upper grades, and you say, 'Oh, in kindergarten that parent was always at the school, and in first grade you saw that parent, while in second grade you saw a little less of that parent.' I've seen it go up through the grades, and I've seen a child from kindergarten here go to the upper grades, the parents think, 'Well, OK, they're getting more mature, they don't need me there.' That's not true, they need them there, even just to say 'You're doing great, I'm really proud of you,' even just to give the teacher some encouragement. I see growth in their child, but they tend to disappear, and then in middle school, you don't see them at all, unless the child has some problem, and then they come up for a parent conference. So I think having parents involved also helps the kids in all that they're learning. Really I do. So if we can get more parents to participate..."*

Cooperation is another value that underlies much of what occurs in Room 7, but it is tempered by an Anglo overlay of the value of working independently. Children are often asked to help each other with their work: "Marisol, when you're finished coloring, can you help Cristóbal?" but may be reprimanded if they do the same spontaneously: "Inés, I don't want to see how much you can help Nina." They are reminded not to look at each other's papers during a test:

*"No quiero ver ojos mirando los papeles de otros,"*  ("I don't want to see eyes looking at other people's papers,")

but Matilde often ends up giving them help herself, as in the hint given on a spelling test for the word *lápiz* (pencil):

*"Si las palabras llevan acentos, Uds. tienen que escribirlas."*  ("If the words have accents, you have to write them.")

Appearances are important in Matilde's classroom, just as they are in most Hispanic cultures.

*"Yo siempre les digo que siempre tienen que hacer su mejor trabajo."*  ("I always tell you that you always have to do your best work.")

The emphasis on neatness and correctness is especially apparent in work that is to be displayed or shared with others. *"They get caught up in doing their work and don't think about the quality of the work they're doing,"* Matilde says. *"A lot of times I let them do it the way they want to. Then they look at somebody else's book and they don't like theirs. They want the one that's nicer."*

Personal appearance is also important. Matilde always looks neat, professional, and coordinated. Most of the children, most of the time, are neat and clean. Their clothing varies from Power Rangers tee shirts to color-coordinated outfits. Camilo's print sports shirts always match his pants. Fatima could be a second-grade fashion model, with her black cowboy boots, tight-fitting blue jeans, neatly braided pony tail and black leather book bag. Marisol likes to have everything from her socks to her hair ribbon all the same color. One day she sports light blue and white striped overall shorts, a bluish turtleneck, blue socks, and a blue hair ribbon, but none of the shades of blue match.

Other aspects of Matilde's value system seem to be more influenced by middle-class Anglo values: Don't watch TV too much:

*"Mijito, tienes que dejar de mirar tanto la televisión. Él está cansado, a lo mejor se pasó la noche, hasta la una o las dos, mirando la televisión, porque él es travieso, cuando se acuesta su madre, él se levanta para mirar la televisión."*  ("Honey, you have to stop watching so much TV. He's tired, I bet he spent all night, until one or two o'clock, watching TV, because he's naughty, when his mother goes to bed, he gets up to watch TV.")

Don't play Atari games too much:

*"Yo creo que Uds. están jugando juegos demasiado. No estén*  ("I think that you guys are playing those games too much.

| | |
|---|---|
| *jugando mucho, por favor, cada quince minutos se levantan para descansar los ojos y las manos también porque es demasiado."* | Don't be playing so much, please, every fifteen minutes get up to rest your eyes and your hand too because it's too much.") |

Don't spend all your money.

| | |
|---|---|
| *"¿Compraste qué? ¿Pasaste mucho tiempo en las tiendas? Gastando billetes en vez de ahorrando."* | ("You bought what? Did you spend a lot of time in the stores? Spending money instead of saving.") |

In spite of the fact that the children are from many different Hispanic cultures there is a shared feeling of "we-ness" in the classroom, provided by commonalities of culture across various Hispanic countries and by the common language. When the cafeteria workers complain that Matilde's students throw away a lot of food, she approaches the issue from the point of view of "Latin" food.

Incorporating
Culture,
p. 119.

| | |
|---|---|
| *"Es otra queja, que están botando demasiada comida. Tienen que comer toda la comida. Aquí no estamos cocinando comida latina. No es arroz con habichuelas, no es chuletas. Es comida americana, y tienen que aprender a comerla. Tienen que aprender a apreciar y a comer de todo."* | ("That's another complaint, that you guys are throwing away too much food. You have to eat all your food. We're not cooking Latin food here. It's not beans and rice, it's not chops. It's American food, and you have to learn to eat it. You have to learn to appreciate and to eat everything.") |

Matilde's sense of "we-ness" is also reflected in her belief that her classroom is loud. It has been observed that people talk louder in Hispanic cultures than in Anglo cultures, and Matilde thinks this is true of her classroom. *"We tend to be loud in this classroom. I've noticed that with bilingual children, so I try to remind them, and to keep myself in check, too. When we have parents come in, they're loud, too, you know. In the homes, it's the same thing."* It does no good to point out to Matilde that her classroom is one of the quietest and calmest in the school. She believes that *"when we work with Hispanic children we tend to talk loud."*

*Observe cultural practices in a bilingual classroom, including overt references to culture and implicit ways in which culture affects what happens in the classroom. Compare your observations with Matilde's classroom and suggest reasons for similarities and differences.*

Observation

This is only one of several seeming contradictions inherent in Matilde's teaching. She calls herself a **whole language** teacher and uses many whole language techniques, yet much of her reading and writing instruction has very little focus on meaning. She says she likes to have children actively participate in their own learning, and her students get very involved in art projects and in creating **big books,** but they have no voice in what they are going to learn or how they are going to learn it. She is aware of the power of high expectations and effectively uses that to shape her students' behavior, but the same high expectations are not communicated about the children's achievement. She has termed herself a "reluctant" teacher who got into teaching by accident and is still not always sure that she wants to be a teacher, yet her enjoyment of her students is obvious in everything she does. She calls herself a disciplinarian, and her students are very well behaved, but they are also very familiar with her. *"Ever since I've been a teacher, kids have always called me by my first name. I feel more comfortable with that than 'Miss Ríos.' I don't know, there's something about 'Miss Ríos.' This year the kids started calling me 'Matt,' and I said 'OK, that's fine, no problem,' because they're always respectful, they're never disrespectful, so there's no problem whatsoever. Sometimes I think they get a little bit too familiar, you know, they talk a lot, and with some of the things they say, I wonder if I'm supposed to draw a line on this or what? Or do I continue to react to it? Sometimes I'm in those situations, you know, like when Ángela called me gorda (fat). Am I supposed to react to that? Am I supposed to say something? And then it doesn't bother me, and I say, 'OK, that's fine. You're right, I eat too much, yo como mucho, me gusta la comida' (I eat a lot, I like to eat')."*

When asked what advice she would have for a beginning bilingual teacher, Matilde responded with three things: Be sure you really care to work in the classroom, because being a bilingual teacher is double duty. Be sure that you are constantly renewing yourself, and finding out what's the latest information, the latest methodologies for working with children. And be sure that you're sure of yourself, and don't forget who you are as you work with the children.

Matilde's third recommendation may reflect her own uncertainty about her career. She has never been convinced that she wants to be a teacher. She sometimes says to her husband, "Do I look like a teacher?" and also wonders about the children, "Do they consider me their teacher?" If she ever decides that she doesn't really want to be a teacher, she will probably leave the classroom and do something else. In the meantime, she takes courses, goes to conferences, and reads a lot to keep up on the best ways of working with bilingual children. Her implementation of what she learns is filtered through all of her previous beliefs and experiences. In everything she does she is herself; good-natured, good-humored, willing to try anything.

It may be that what appear to be contradictions to an outsider are not really contradictions to Matilde. Her implementation of whole language teaching is based on her beliefs and her experiences, which have changed over the years and will continue to change. Each person viewing her classroom or reading this description of her teaching will evaluate what Matilde does according to his or her own beliefs about teaching and learning. The ultimate test of any teacher's practices is whether her students learned more because she taught this way than they would have learned if she had taught in any other way. For these children, in this classroom, only Matilde can answer that.

# FRAMEWORKS

*Bilingual children learn
in the same ways as other children*

*The titles of the nine themes in the Frameworks section are in a sense "maxims" that reflect my beliefs about how all children learn best. Would you change this list in any way? If so, how and why? If not, why not?*

Bilingual children begin school full of curiosity, eager to learn, and anxious to please their parents and teachers by doing well. Some bilingual children are able to maintain their curiosity, their eagerness, their desire to please; they generally succeed in school. Others seem to lose these qualities along the way; they do not do well in school and may end up dropping out. The reasons are complex, often involving societal forces that are beyond the capacity of individual classroom teachers to remedy. However, there is much that individual teachers can do to make classrooms more exciting places for bilingual children (and for *all* children), thus expanding and building on the curiosity, eagerness, and desire to please that young children bring with them to school.

I believe there are two major factors that turn children off to the excitement of learning. One is the assumption, made by most teachers, that children arrive at school with certain competencies; those children who don't have the expected competencies are often reminded in subtle and not-so-subtle ways that they are deficient. Children from backgrounds that are linguistically and culturally different from the "mainstream" school population may not have the competencies that the school expects. When children first come to school they are supposed to know colors and numbers and have some sense of letters. They are supposed to know what reading and writing are and what uses they have. They are supposed to want to learn to read. Don Holdaway has called this a "literacy set," a concept that includes motivational factors ("high expectations of print"), linguistic factors ("familiarity with written dialect in oral form"), operational factors ("essential strategies for handling written language"), and orthographic factors ("knowledge of the conventions of print") (1979, p. 62). The idea of "literacy set" is a powerful tool to help explain why initial reading seems so easy

Journal

Pp. 13-20 chronicle the daily activities of three children in Matilde's classroom.

for some children and so difficult for others.

Children who begin school without this "literacy set" need to acquire the concepts that form it. Holdaway has provided techniques for doing that. It wasn't until I read *Foundations of Literacy* that I realized that the size of a **big book** was not meant simply to appeal to children; it was meant to allow all the children in a group to see the print. Holdaway created big books to replicate the kind of situation that preschool children experience in story reading with their parents, which is where much of the "literacy set" is developed. The children's favorite stories are read to them repeatedly, and the children are soon able to recreate the stories from the pictures and from their knowledge of the text. If, in the process, they are also able to see the text, they begin to associate certain sounds with certain marks on the paper, and reading has begun.

Many of Holdaway's techniques are widely used in holistic approaches to literacy instruction. In other approaches, however, children are instructed in decontextualized reading skills before they have acquired the basic knowledge of functions of print that would give meaning to those skills. Because they are not allowed to read until they master the skills, and the skills are meaningless without the ability to read, children often acquire neither reading skills nor reading ability.

This does not mean that instruction in literacy skills is not needed. Another aspect of Holdaway's work that is very appealing is the idea that skills can be directly taught within a meaning-based approach to reading. Some children can teach themselves all the reading skills they need without any instruction in consonant sounds, syllables, guessing from context, predicting, or any other decoding or comprehension strategies. I call this the ability to "make connections." These children figure it out for themselves. Other children can't make the connections by themselves, however—they need a teacher's assistance. We cannot ignore reading skills with such students and assume that they will learn them on their own if they simply read enough. Holdaway's work provides excellent suggestions for modeling and teaching skills within the most meaningful framework possible; a child's favorite story.

The other major factor that turns children off to the excitement of learning is the amount of sheer nonsense they are required to put up with in school. Bilingual children, in particular, may be exposed to more mundane, repetitive work than other children because it is felt by many teachers that they need more instruction in "**basic skills**" than other children. Basic skills are conceived of as incremental pieces of language and mathematics, each of which must be mastered before moving on to the next. Because these small pieces of language and mathematics make no sense in and of themselves, they are more difficult to learn than the larger, more meaningful pieces that are embedded in rich contexts. In addition, the rote, meaningless way much basic skills instruction is carried out is less conducive to cognitive development and critical thinking than are more challenging forms of instruction.

Carole Edelsky (1991, p. 69) has termed the ability to do well with this kind of instruction "Skill in Instructional Nonsense" (SIN). SIN is the ability to tolerate instruction that has no intrinsic meaning or purpose, and which is presented to children only so they can practice a skill that the school considers necessary in order to learn to read, write, or do mathematics problems. Adults would rebel if asked to do even a small portion of the boring, senseless, valueless work that children routinely do in schools, but many children are able to develop a high tolerance for instructional nonsense.

Children who succeed in developing skill in instructional nonsense have two characteristics. One is the ability to make connections on their own, and the other is their willingness to go along with instructional nonsense simply because the teacher asks them to do so. They do not rebel at the meaninglessness of the tasks they're asked to do because they have learned to accept whatever schools ask of them.

Children who fail to develop skill in instructional nonsense lack one or both of these characteristics. They may be able to make the connections but are simply not willing or able to put up with the nonsense, or they may accept the nonsense but not be able to make the connections. Making connections without assistance requires knowing the language of the school, whether that language is your first or second language, and being able to use that language in literate ways. It requires the ability to form a concept based on experiences in school, extract that concept from the context in which it was formed, and apply it to other situations. Accepting instructional nonsense requires a willingness to conform to school expectations and to accept boredom as the price one must pay for success. It also requires accepting the assumption that school success can lead to other kinds of success, which can be problematic for many bilingual children.

In a study of bilingual children's writing, Carole Edelsky (1986) demonstrated that bilingual children can achieve school success in classrooms in which the curriculum consists of authentic literacy activities, and in which they are evaluated on their performance on these authentic tasks. Her research counteracts many of the "myths," as she calls them, that contribute to the notion that bilingual children cannot succeed at school. Some of these myths include the belief that bilingual children's native language is not well developed when they come to school, so they have no basis on which to build a second language; the belief that their nonliterate backgrounds inhibit the acquisition of literacy in either language; and the belief that their native language interferes with the acquisition and production of English. Contrary to these myths, Edelsky's data show language strengths rather than language deficits: bilingualism as an asset rather than a limitation; first language literacy being applied to rather than interfering with writing in the second language; and literacy being acquired through constructing, revising, and abandoning hypotheses, rather than through mastery of discrete skills in a linear progression. Edelsky's research shows that under the proper conditions, bilingual children can develop age-appropriate levels of literacy in both their first and second languages. If they don't, it is often due to the use of inappropriate tasks to teach reading and writing, rather than to anything being "wrong" with the children.

Many people believe that schools are set up as gatekeepers to ensure that certain classes of children succeed while others fail. Although there may be some truth to this assertion, it is a political question beyond the scope of this book. However, if children are failing in school because of their backgrounds, it is because not enough individual teachers have changed their practices. There may be gates that try to keep certain children from succeeding in school, but individual teachers can do a great deal to keep those gates open. We don't have to blame the children who come to school with backgrounds that are different from what we expect. We don't have to continue to provide them with a steady diet of instructional nonsense. We must have the courage of our convictions that all children can learn, and teach accordingly.

Classroom
Research,
p. 115.

Every child comes to school curious about letters, words, numbers, people who live differently than they do, frogs (or butterflies, machines, dinosaurs...). Under the proper conditions, this curiosity is transformed into the ability to read, write, do mathematics, understand social issues, and be scientists. When it isn't, it should not be assumed that the children can't succeed in school because they are bilingual (or for whatever other reason). It should be assumed that they can succeed if the school provides the proper conditions. Then we should find out what those conditions are and implement them.

Reflection

*Do the conditions provided in Matilde's classroom give the three children described on pages xx-xx an optimal chance to succeed in school? List both positive and negative conditions for school success that exist in that classroom.*

## Suggested Readings:

*Key Works:* Two books that influenced my thinking about how children learn are Holdaway (1979) and Edelsky (1986). Donald Holdaway calls his book "a child-watcher's guide to literacy" (p. 7); he looks at early literacy from a developmental point of view and explains how to provide the supportive environment that will capitalize on children's potential to teach themselves. Carole Edelsky reports on a year-long study of bilingual children's writing; she provides counterevidence to many of the common deficit-based myths about bilingual children.

Henry Trueba's (1989) book about educating language minority students for the twenty-first century begins with the premise that minority children have the ability to do well in school, and examines some of the reasons why they often do not. He also makes suggestions for classroom practice, curriculum design, and teacher preparation.

Smith et al. (1993) have written a thought-provoking article that challenges the very notion of "failure" in school. They suggest that attempts to explain school failure actually promote its proliferation; if we view failure as a fabrication, learning will become easy for all children.

# Children learn when they are doing something that has an authentic purpose

*Most children throughout the history of schooling have learned by doing exercises that have no other purpose than practice. Doesn't this contradict my claim that activities must have an authentic purpose that goes beyond practice? Examine and record your own beliefs about the necessity of authenticity in learning activities, particularly literacy learning activities.*

Journal

So much of what we ask children to do in school has no purpose other than to learn and practice a skill. This contrasts with much authentic learning in the world beyond school, which is done through observation or apprenticeship. In an observation model of learning, the learners watch until they can do the task themselves or produce the product. In an apprenticeship model, the master supervises the accomplishment of the task or the production of the product to ensure that costly mistakes are not made. In both cases the learners know that what they are working on is real, and therefore must be done to the best of their ability.

Most of what children are asked to do in schools is not real. It is all simply practice so that presumably, at some future time when students are faced with real tasks, they will be able to do them. The children know this, so exhortations from the teacher to "do your best" become meaningless. If nobody is going to see a child's story except the teacher and perhaps the few other children who bother to look at the bulletin board where work is posted, there is little incentive to write a good story. If the children are not sure whether they have spelled a word correctly, they can simply wait for the teacher to tell them whether it's right or wrong. That's easier than figuring it out for themselves, and since the task they are doing has no other purpose than to do what the teacher says, it doesn't make any difference if they do it wrong in the first place.

Compare this situation with one in which children are writing books that are going to be used as reading materials by another class. This is an authentic product that must be correct because children shouldn't try to learn to read from books that don't have margins, paragraphs, or spaces between words. It becomes important to get the capital letters right because these books will become models for other children who are learning to write.

This example is obviously an authentic purpose for writing, but not all authentic purposes are so easily described. One of the meanings of authenticity in language is that there should be a reason for producing language that goes beyond practice. In other words, authentic language has an authentic function. In the real world, language has a multitude of functions. We use language to clarify, request, apologize, empathize, criticize, convince, explain, invite, praise, slander, motivate—the list is endless. Practice is also one of the functions of language. If I'm going to deliver a speech, I will practice it beforehand. There is nothing wrong with using language for practice. However, practice must be for an authentic task, and it must be limited to situations in which practice for that kind of task is needed. This is not the same as unnecessary practice of discrete language items. Yet in many language classrooms, that makes up the totality of language use in the classroom.

One example of this kind of meaningless practice occurs when second language students are being taught to speak a language. What they do in class normally consists of nothing more than talking about things that everybody already knows and can anticipate responses to, but in a different code. Sometimes language teachers try to provide meaningful language by ensuring that students talk about things that their hearers or readers don't already know. They ask questions about what students like best, or what they did the previous day. "What did you do last night?" is certainly a more meaningful question than "Is this a book?" The problem here is the discourse pattern. The teacher asks a question, a student answers, and the teacher provides feedback. Then the teacher goes on to another student, asking the same question. In real discourse we don't provide minimal, perfunctory feedback to a conversational partner's response and then move on to ask another partner the same question. This initiation-response-feedback (IRF) pattern also puts the student in the position of always answering questions posed by the teacher. Occasionally students may work in pairs so they also get practice asking questions, but this still provides a very limited repertoire of language functions. When do students get a chance to disagree, to express concern, to encourage, to express displeasure? If classroom language is to be usable outside the classroom, it must include the full range of functions of language students are likely to encounter there. In order to develop fully their first *and* second languages, bilingual children need extensive opportunities to use both languages in meaningful, functional situations.

The same concerns also apply to written language. Worksheets on which children fill in the blanks with vocabulary words from a box or decide whether to put periods or question marks at the ends of sentences reflect no authentic function of written language. Authentic written language conveys information and feelings and directives, just as spoken language does. Having students write in journals every day can be an authentic use of written language, but only if somebody reads what they have written, or if keeping a journal is their own choice. If letters are written, they should be mailed. If stories are written, they should be read. None of these forms of writing should be used exclusively for the purpose of learning to write—that misappropriates their natural functions. A journal is not the proper place for a teacher to insist that all spelling and punctuation be correct. This detracts not only from the child's efforts to convey meaning, but also turns what should be a pleasant experience into an unpleasant task. Frank Smith wrote that "Wise teachers avoid any kind of 'instruction' that reduces the amount of writing children do. These teachers want children to learn to spell, punctuate, capitalize, and so forth, but they recognize that this learning occurs in other circumstances (and primarily through reading) rather than through obstacles in the process of writing" (1986, p. 214).

Of course, children can learn to spell and punctuate correctly through journal writing. That kind of learning occurs most effectively when children watch the modeling done by a teacher who is also engaged in journal writing. If the modeling is done in a **dialogue journal**, in which the teacher responds to each journal entry made by the child, then the forms that the teacher has modeled become immediately available for use by the child in his or her next entry. With

Teachers' Voices

Uses of literacy in Matilde's classroom are described on pp. 20-30.

Investigations

Case Study, p. 115.

beginning writers, teachers often respond to children's journals in their presence so the modeling can occur with comments about why the teacher does things in certain ways.

In the case of reading, it is more difficult to determine what authenticity means. Some people claim that in order to be authentic, reading must be self-selected. However, much work-related reading done by adults in the real world is not self-selected. Throughout their academic careers students will have to do a great deal of reading that will not be self-selected, but is surely authentic. Perhaps a better way to look at the issue of authenticity in reading is to return to the concept of practicing a skill versus performing a task. Authentic reading should be done for some reason other than simply to practice reading. Authentic reasons for reading can include personal enjoyment, reading to learn something, or reading because the teacher wants the whole class to discuss a particular story.

Authentic reading also means reading authentic texts. Authentic texts do not have controlled vocabulary. Authentic texts are not written to give readers practice using certain **sound-symbol correspondences**. **Shared reading** techniques, in which the teacher reads a favorite story repeatedly to the students, eliminate the need for controlled vocabulary. Repetition can be accomplished in a meaningful way by using **predictable** texts, and any specific sound-symbol correspondences that children may need practice with can easily be found in an authentic story.

A moving testimony to the power of authenticity in language learning was included in the plenary speech given by Shirley Brice Heath at the 1984 TESOL Conference (Heath, 1985). Heath described work she had done in collaboration with a high school English teacher, most of whose ninth-grade basic English students had previously been in special education classes. The teacher shared the students' work and her own field notes with Heath, who wrote letters to the students and made them her "associate **ethnographers**." During the first semester of the program the students corresponded with college-bound junior and senior English classes and learned about ethnography. During the second semester Heath wrote to them, asking them to collect data on their uses of language. They were to take field notes, analyze data, send the data to her, and respond to her questions.

Heath claims that she treated these low-functioning students in exactly the same way she would treat her graduate research assistants, except that at the beginning she personalized her letters to them. Otherwise she wrote as she would to a university-level colleague. If the students sent data that were not in usable form, or if Heath disagreed with their interpretations, she explained why she disagreed, what she needed, and what the students should do. The two sides negotiated with each other in writing, challenging interpretations, providing evidence, and finally coming to joint conclusions.

Heath reported that all of these students moved out of basic English into regular English classes at the end of the year, and two of them moved into honors classes. I later found out that almost all of them completed high school, and several went on to two- and four-year colleges. These students had been given responsibility for completing an important task. That task required that they be able to comprehend what they read in the letters from Heath and express themselves coherently and correctly in writing to her. They responded to that task as they had never responded to years of remedial instruction in the "skills" that

Investigations

Discuss with a colleague arguments against the position that literacy tasks in school must have authentic purposes.

Smith's book is also discussed in Technology, on p. 90, and in Assessment, on p. 103.

supposedly go into reading with comprehension and writing with clarity.

Another powerful plea for meaningful instruction comes from Frank Smith. His book *Insult to Intelligence: The Bureaucratic Invasion of Our Classrooms* (1986) has shaped my thinking about how schools should function. It has implications not only for authenticity of function in language instruction but also for technology use and for assessment of students.

If I remember nothing else about Frank Smith's book twenty years from now, I will remember the r-bbit (pronounced "are-bit"). The r-bbit is a creature that inhabits workbooks and computer programs, "teaching" children the innumerable "skills" they supposedly need to be able to read and write, and then assessing their mastery of those skills. The book is a scathing indictment of how American education has been taken over by programmatic instructional materials, full of r-bbits and other similar creatures that have been conceived and designed by outside "experts" who are not even teachers, and forced on teachers who should know better. With vivid examples and clear logic, Smith demonstrates the nonsensical nature of much of what goes on in schools, the difference between this programmatic nonsense and real learning, and the disempowerment of teachers as they fall into the trap of using materials that tell them what to do and what to say at all times.

Smith says that teachers can combat this "insult to intelligence" by learning to tell the difference between the r-bbit and real learning, working to get rid of the r-bbit as much as possible, and protecting themselves and their students from whatever nonsense they can't get rid of by being honest about what it is and why they are doing it. Fill-in-the-blank exercises and multiple-choice tests have become so much a part of American schools that many teachers don't even think to question why they use them. When they do think about it, teachers realize that the most beneficial kinds of activities for all students are those that had previously been considered "enrichment" for the more advanced students who finish their skills exercises early. As more and more time is given to these "enrichment" activities, less time is available for skills practice, and students end up learning more. Instructional nonsense that cannot be eliminated is recognized as such. When students are asked to do something that has no authentic purpose, they are not led to believe that it is a task vital to their learning.

What does a classroom based on authentic language use look like? Talk in such a classroom has to do with the work that goes on in the room. It is a negotiation of meaning among teacher and children revolving around what is going to be learned, what activities will be done, what things mean, how we know what we know, and sharing what we have learned and how we learned it. It is rooted in both the content that the children are learning and the procedures used to learn it. It is democratic, with children having both time to contribute and freedom to say what they think. It is not controlled by the teacher.

Reading in such a classroom has a myriad of functions. Children read for pleasure: picture books, story books, chapter books, poems, songs. They read to follow directions: experiments, recipes, procedures written down by the teacher or by other students. They read to gain information: reference books, textbooks, story books, reports written by other students. They read the same sources to confirm information acquired through other means. They read for social purposes: notes to each other, notices on bulletin boards, dialogue journals, letters to pen pals or E-mail pals.

Writing also has a myriad of functions, many of which reflect the reading functions listed above: for pleasure, to provide directions, to convey information, for social purposes. Children write to find out what they know and think, just as adults do. They write to share with others something they believe is worth telling. They write so they won't forget, they write so someone else won't forget, they write for the sheer pleasure of playing with words on paper.

In authentic classrooms, science, mathematics, and social studies are not just subjects in a textbook. Textbooks are used to gain information, but the information is not gained for its own sake. It is put to use in some way on an authentic project. It takes a lot of practice with addition and multiplication to figure out how much money the school made by collecting soda bottles to return for the deposit. It becomes very important to know what city and state you live in, and what the difference between a city and a state is, when you're writing a travel brochure about your city and state to send to a class in Australia. Proper procedures for data collection and handling (not to mention map-reading skills) become crucial when you are going to test water samples from all over the city to determine which areas of the city have water quality problems.

Two books that provide excellent examples of authentic classrooms as I have described them are *Inventing a Classroom* (Whitmore and Crowell, 1994) and *Constructing Knowledge Together* (Wells and Chang-Wells, 1992). Whitmore and Crowell describe a bilingual **whole language** classroom in which the students invent the curriculum and show how language and content instruction interact to contribute to the development of both. Wells and Chang-Wells describe a mainstream classroom that contains many second language learners and show how talk about cognitively demanding tasks leads to literate thinking.

Children learn what they are taught. If we teach them to do exercises, they will learn to do exercises. Some may also learn to do the authentic tasks that the exercises are supposed to prepare them for, but this usually happens through preforming authentic tasks outside school. For those who aren't able to transfer the "skills" they learn in school to real tasks, it may be that they have few opportunities outside school to do authentic tasks, or it may be that they have simply rebelled against the uselessness of the exercises and given up on learning. Some of these children may be motivated by a strong desire to accomplish something later, and may then succeed at tasks that are seemingly beyond their capabilities. Children who fail mathematics in school can learn to keep perfect records for their paper routes. Students who are barely able to read in school one day can decipher the legalese of a contract. Others who have great difficulty writing later master the genre of business letters when their success depends on it. In all these cases, the key to their success is authenticity.

We are leaving our students' futures up to chance if we rely on the real world to supply the authenticity they need in order to make sense out of what they learn in school. It doesn't have to be so. Schools can easily be made into places of authentic learning if teachers are willing to take charge of their students' learning themselves, instead of leaving it to curriculum and materials developers. It is time to banish the nonsense from our classrooms.

Additional examples of authentic science, math, and social studies activities can be found in Learn by Doing, pp. 73-79.

Classroom Research, p. 116.

Reflection

*Suggest ways in which the reading and writing activities in Matilde's classroom could be made more authentic.*

## Suggested Readings:

*Key Works:* Although the books by Heath (1985) and Smith (1986) are very different, they both had a major impact on me. Heath describes two teacher-researcher-student linkages that enabled students to go beyond basic literacy skills to literate understanding about language. Smith attacks the "ritualistic teaching of nonsense" (p. xx) that is embodied in much basic skills instruction and describes alternatives to programmatic instruction controlled by outside "experts."

Two books that describe how to create the kind of authentic environment I advocate are Enright and McCloskey (1988) and Pérez and Torres-Guzmán (1996). The former is addressed to mainstream classroom teachers, the latter to Spanish-English bilingual teachers, but both books would be useful to teachers in any situation who want to move in that direction. Spanish bilingual teachers may also want to consult Freeman and Freeman (1997), who describe traditional methods for teaching Spanish reading, holistic/constructivist alternatives, patterns of writing development in Spanish, and ways to combine native and second language reading and writing to develop biliteracy.

Gordon Wells and Gen Ling Chang-Wells (1992) report on a collaborative research study in four schools with large multilingual populations. They include many examples of language being used as a tool for learning and for sharing what has been learned, and show how this kind of literate oral language use supports and facilitates written language use.

# Children learn by doing

*To what extent do most teachers you have worked with or observed engage their students in learning by doing? What factors contribute to teachers' decisions to teach in this or some other way?*

Journal

There are certain things that children can only learn by doing themselves. In the acquisition of reading and writing skills, schools give lip service to the need for learning by doing. There is little argument against the saying that "Children learn to read by reading and learn to write by writing." In practice, however, much "reading" instruction consists of learning the "sounds" of letters and letter combinations and learning comprehension skills such as "finding the main idea." Practice in "reading" may consist of filling in missing letters in a word, underlining the details that support the main idea, or choosing the correct answer among several in response to a question about a paragraph. Much "writing" instruction consists of learning to use capital and small letters correctly, paragraph indentation, proper punctuation, and correct spelling. Practice in "writing" may consist of copying a text written on the chalkboard; combining sentences written by somebody else; or correcting errors in spelling, punctuation, and capitalization on a worksheet.

In teaching mathematics, schools appear to acknowledge the need to learn by doing. Children practice computations, practice more computations, and then practice more computations. They also practice solving "story problems." However, children don't really learn to "do mathematics" unless they experience a problem-solving approach to understanding mathematical concepts.

Less attention is given in science and social studies to the need to do in order to learn. Some schools acknowledge the existence of the scientific method and encourage experimentation in science classes, but most of the experiments are pre-planned by the teacher. Students may be encouraged to suggest hypotheses, but the teacher knows the results of the experiments before they are carried out. This is not at all what real scientists do. Social studies is normally seen as a body of knowledge to be acquired, usually by reading a textbook, although films, videos, filmstrips, and realia can substitute for or even replace the textbook, especially in the lower grades. In spite of these more experiential materials, however, learning social studies remains a matter of coming to understand information that others have collected.

There are increasing calls for mathematics, science, and social studies to be taught in ways that will allow children to "do" them as well as learn about them. "Doing" mathematics requires much more than practicing computations and artificial story problems. There is little point in learning to solve a problem such as "Farmer Brown has twenty acres of corn. He gets 150 bushels of corn from each acre. How many bushels of corn does Farmer Brown get?" when children don't know how big an acre is or how much corn fits in a bushel. The main lesson most children learn from problems such as these is to dislike story problems. Children need to do the kinds of mathematical problems encountered in the real world. They also need to understand the mathematical concepts that

Examples of how these subjects are taught in Matilde's classroom are found on pp. 31-37.

underlie computation.

In science, rather than achieve superficial mastery of unrelated facts and definitions, students should learn the scientific process by working to discover phenomena as scientists do. There must be genuine experimentation, rather than the kind in which the outcome is predetermined by the teacher or the textbook. It is true that not all necessary scientific information can be acquired through experimentation; there is simply too much knowledge and not enough time in which to discover it. However, a solid understanding of how scientific knowledge is discovered can provide a strong foundation on which to later add additional knowledge about things discovered by others.

"Doing" social studies includes such a broad range of methodologies that most teachers would be unsure of how to go about having their students begin to act like social scientists. The techniques used by historians, geographers, anthropologists, sociologists, and political scientists vary widely. One approach that has been used to give students the experience of "doing" social studies is to have them become **ethnographers**. The ethnographic skills of observing, recording, and analyzing behavior in particular contexts are used in many of the disciplines within the social sciences.

In spite of the preponderance of textbook-oriented instruction in mathematics, science, and social studies, there are enough examples of students learning by doing to show how easily it can be done. An example from social studies is Edelsky, Altwerger, and Flores's (1991) description of a Chapter One Resource Room in which the children become archeologists and anthropologists after finding some pottery shards on the school grounds. The students hypothesize about what kinds of utensils the shards came from and compare their hypotheses to reference books. They develop questions to ask an archeologist who comes to talk to them. Since not all the children get to hear him speak, a tape of his talk becomes a resource for other children in their search for answers to questions. They research the history of the Anasazi Indians who once lived in that area and make a time line. They keep track of their own activities and accomplishments at the various centers set up around the room, as they work independently and in small groups to find the answers to their own questions. When they discover that some present-day Indians live in pick-up trucks instead of homes, that becomes the topic for a whole-class discussion.

More information on critical pedagogy can be found in Involvement, pp. 86-89.

An approach to social studies that combines **whole language** and **critical pedagogy** is advocated by Freeman and Freeman (1991). They describe a general paradigm shift in education from the **transmission** of knowledge to the active construction of knowledge. In social studies this means less reliance on textbooks and more on authentic documents; less reliance on lectures and worksheets and more on active student involvement; less reliance on the transmission of facts and more on using students' backgrounds and interests. The **whole language** movement has been identified with the elements of this paradigm shift, but neither the paradigm shift nor the whole language movement necessarily incorporates a critical perspective. The critical perspective comes from Paulo Freire's (1970) philosophy, which includes a focus on planning for social action. His problem-posing approach has been described by Wallerstein (1987). In the first phase the teacher listens to students to discover issues that can serve as generative themes. In the second phase the teacher promotes dialogue through asking questions and providing information that promotes critical thinking, but does not impose his or her own answers or solutions. In the third phase students learn to see themselves as social and political beings through actions both within and outside class. One of the examples given by the Freemans is of a class that read about a new city ordinance requiring the use of water meters to conserve water. The students surveyed community members about their views on water conservation, developed a position paper on the issue, and wrote letters to the editor of the local newspaper.

Peterson's (1991) account of his implementation of critical pedagogy in a fifth-grade bilingual classroom provides many examples of learning social studies by doing social studies. Peterson helped his students develop a critical perspective on society through critiquing the curriculum and textbooks. Students learned that textbooks may not always be right or may distort the truth through omissions. The biases of maps that put the equator two-thirds of the way down from the top of the map and make Europe larger than South America were exposed. Stereotypes were examined, with one result being that Peterson's students got angry when their little brothers and sisters made feathered Indian headbands at Thanksgiving. The nature of knowledge as socially constructed was examined by the students reading several newspaper or magazine articles that reflected different views on the same topic. Action occurred when Peterson's students went on marches, testified before the city council, and wrote to Congress. Projects that are less political in nature are also options, such as adopting a section of a beach or a river and keeping it clean, or raising money for famine or disaster relief.

Peterson found that one way of helping students become critical about the oppression that exists in society is to bring the world into the classroom and take the classroom into the world, thus allowing students to better reflect on their own lives. After watching the movie version of *The Grapes of Wrath*, the students went on a field trip to hear César Chavez speak, and then interviewed local workers who were on strike. As Peterson says, "they learned more during their half-hour interview than they had in years of social studies lessons" (p. 162). Their interest in wages, strikes, and unions led to an examination of their own parents' wages, work sites, and union membership; "grievance" became a spelling word and they began looking for grievances in their own lives.

These fifth-grade inner-city bilingual students no longer accept everything they read or are told. They have the skills to critically reflect on how both present and past events affect their lives. They know that society can be changed through action. They will be much better prepared to deal with the complexity of modern times—which is the aim of social studies education—than students who understand the social structure but don't understand how to change it.

In the field of science, one example of learning by doing comes from a program in which linguistic minority students in inner-city classrooms were taught sophisticated forms of scientific reasoning by treating them as scientists and giving them the resources and support necessary to conduct scientific inquiries (Rosebery, Warren & Conant, 1992). The project was called *Cheche Konnen*, which means "search for knowledge" in Haitian Creole. One of the studies that was carried out was done by a seventh- and eighth-grade Haitian bilingual class. They began with the question of why the drinking fountain on the third floor of their school was considered the "best." To answer this question, the students conducted a blind taste test, which revealed that the fountain on the first floor actually had better-tasting water. This led to an inquiry about the discrepancy between taste and preference, and another into the causes of the differences in taste. Throughout the process students had to form hypotheses, collect and analyze data, compare results, and come to conclusions.

Wells and Chang-Wells (1992) describe a classroom in which a group of third- and fourth-grade children had just watched some chickens hatch. In most classrooms, such an event would trigger teacher-directed discussion about how the chicks got out of the eggs, what they were eating while they were inside the eggs, or how they got inside the eggs. In this classroom, however, the birth of the chicks triggered small-group investigations, with children trying to find out the chicks' genders; weighing, recording, and graphing weight increases; measuring the length of the baby chicks' toes; experimenting to find out what the chicks were most likely to peck at; and constructing a house for a chick, complete with central heating.

Giving children time to investigate their own interests always brings up the question of "covering the curriculum." The argument is that if teachers allow children to spend large amounts of time pursuing their own interests, they won't learn everything they should. When curriculum drives a classroom, a school, or a school system, teachers often decide that they must control how the children spend their time. When knowledge of how children learn drives a classroom, a school, or a school system, teachers have more freedom to follow children's interests. There is no question in my mind which way children learn best.

One of my favorite descriptions of "doing" science is Shirley Brice Heath's (1983) description of students becoming ethnographers. Included in a chapter near the end of *Ways with Words*, it has been overshadowed by the importance of the rest of the book and has not received the attention it deserves. The project involved a fifth-grade class of minority students whose first language was a nonstandard dialect of English. Most were reading at or below a second-grade level, and none had ever passed a standardized science unit test in the past. Under Heath's guidance, the students became interested in the work of anthropologists and learned about field methods. For a science unit on plant life they were asked to imagine that they were advisors to an agricultural resource center that was to be set up in their area. Their job was to learn as much as possible about how things were grown locally in order to be able to advise the center on how local concepts of agriculture were like scientific approaches and how they differed. They had to develop their questions, locate the best local farmers and find out what their methods were, and compare those methods with scientific sources. All the information they collected orally from local informants had to be compared with information from another source, either experimental or from science books. The culmination of the unit was a science book that was produced for the next year's class that contained oral histories of the people interviewed, charts comparing local folk concepts of agriculture with scientific concepts, and translations of those folk concepts into scientific concepts.

This project took a qualitative approach to scientific inquiry, having students act as ethnographers of science. Although it differed from the traditional "scientific method" in that hypotheses were not generated at the beginning of the investigation, students were still required to formulate questions, collect data, and draw conclusions from the data. Additionally, all data had to be corroborated from a different kind of source, thus forcing students to develop bibliographic skills in order to consult scientific texts.

The results of this program were impressive. Over half the class scored above 90 percent on the standardized unit test at the end of the project, and nobody failed. Attendance and parental involvement improved. There were many refinements in language skills: reading levels increased and students learned to define vocabulary items and ask questions that would elicit specific information. Perhaps most important, they learned to translate knowledge from the personalized, contextualized, oral style of the community to the depersonalized, decontextualized, written style required in the classroom.

A good example of "doing math" is provided by Davison and Reyner (1992). Their "Whole Mathematics" program begins with having children observe how math is used in their daily lives. From there they go on to use all four language skills in a variety of ways in creating and solving their own story problems. Personal math journals, letters explaining what they are learning, and a group math project of their own design serve to relate the mathematics they are learning to their own lives.

Hudelson (1989) provides a specific example in which a complex concept such as probability is presented in a way that makes it understandable by relating it to everyday events in students' lives. She suggests beginning by having children discuss the chances of everyday events happening, such as seeing a certain kind of car, having a perfect math paper, or a team's winning a football game. The discussion then moves to probability: children decide which of two things is more probable (going swimming in summer or winter; having pizza for breakfast or for lunch). After some practice in categorizing statements as certain, uncertain, or probable (using our brains this week, seeing the sun tomorrow, sleeping eight hours Tuesday night), children can look at mathematical probability through tossing coins and dice and recording the numbers of occurrences of heads, even numbers, or particular numbers.

This example could be expanded to embrace a more critical stance (Shor, 1987; Walsh, 1993), in which probability is used not only as a generative theme but also as an occasion for reflection and action. Students could discuss the probability of winning different kinds of lottery games; investigate their popularity in the community; reflect on the impact of spending money on lottery tickets; and act on their findings in various ways such as writing reports, editorials, letters to the editor, or letters to their families.

Frankenstein (1987) reports on another example of critical mathematics education in which basic math skills were learned and practiced in contexts that challenged the dominant ideology. Among the examples she gives was one in which figures from an article on how much the government spends on the nuclear industry were used to practice working with decimals. Another example involved comparing the amount the government spends on welfare with the amount of money that goes to tax loopholes for the rich. Although most of Frankenstein's examples are not appropriate for elementary school children, some of them would be understandable to children in the middle grades. Alternative topics could be used in the early grades. First graders working with the concepts of greater than and less than could use numbers representing the cost of disposing of a single plastic bottle versus the cost of recycling it. The benefits of recycling could be reinforced by practicing addition using the numbers of empty bottles the children see on the streets on their way to school each day.

In all of these examples children are successfully completing activities that might seem to be beyond their capabilities. The key to their success lies in the authenticity of the tasks, the students' involvement, and the fact that support is provided when children need it. This kind of teaching also gives students the best opportunities possible for meaningful authentic language use, and for cognitive and language development. Cognitive development cannot occur without corresponding language development; therefore everything we ask children to do in school should be appropriate for developing both kinds of skills. This provides for the development of what Cummins (1980) has called Cognitive Academic Language Proficiency (CALP). Cummins has developed several hypotheses that contribute greatly to understanding bilingual language acquisition which any bilingual teacher should be familiar with. I do not discuss them here because they are not essential to the themes in this book. Interested readers are referred to Cummins (1984, 1989).

In this discussion we have seen children acting in ways that resemble real mathematicians, scientists, and social scientists. They are not learning sterile facts out of a textbook, to be forgotten as soon as the class moves on to another topic. Nor are they practicing senseless exercises in order to perhaps be able to do real science, mathematics or social studies at some future time. In learning by doing they will achieve a depth of understanding of the subject not possible in any other way and an interest in the subject that will help them continue to learn about it as they grow.

Activities
Continuum, p. 116.

Classroom
Research, p. 116.

Reflection

*To what extent are Matilde's students "learning by doing" in science, mathematics, and social studies? How could the lessons described be modified to allow for more active student participation?*

## Suggested Readings:

*Key Works:* Vivid accounts of real students "learning by doing" are found in Heath (1983) and Peterson (1991); both have been an inspiration to me in my attempts to improve my own teaching. Heath describes a fifth-grade science class composed mainly of black males who had been tracked into the lowest level of science; using ethnographic techniques to study local agricultural practices, all managed to pass the standardized unit test. Peterson describes his Freirian approach to teaching in a fifth-grade bilingual classroom, including many specific examples of activities he did with his students, as well as the theory behind his practices and the effects on his students' achievement.

Although not written specifically for teachers of bilingual children, three books would be helpful in moving toward "learning by doing" in content area teaching: *Doing What Scientists Do* (Doris, 1991) is a guide to bringing classroom teaching reality closer to the theory of teaching "hands-on" science. *Thinking like Mathematicians* (Rowan and Bourne, 1994) guides teachers in the implementation of the National Council on the Teaching of Mathematics Standards in grades K-4. *Constructing Buildings, Bridges, and Minds* (Young, 1994) describes year-long integrated projects based on social studies themes and culminating in the construction of large-scale models of Washington, D.C., and Latin America.

# Children learn when their teachers believe in them, in themselves, and in what they are doing

**Investigations**

Journal

**Teachers' Voices**

Matilde's methods of teaching are revealed throughout the Teachers' Voices strand. The beliefs underlying those methods are described on pp. 37-43.

*Think of examples you have experienced or observed where teachers' high or low expectations affected student achievement. Think as well of times when teachers used methods that were outdated or discredited but worked for them because of their belief in the methods. Try to explain how beliefs—whether in students or in methods—can have so much power.*

There has long been a great emphasis on methods in the teaching of reading and language. There is the linguistic method, the communicative method, the phonics method, and the direct method. There is the sight word approach, the natural approach, the **language experience approach**, and the **whole language** approach. Don't forget Silent Way, Distar, **Key Words**, and Words in Color. And of course, there are ALM, CLL, ITA, and TPR (Audio-Lingual Method, Community Language Learning, Initial Teaching Alphabet, and Total Physical Response). Various people have unsuccessfully tried to distinguish between method and approach (Anthony, 1963; Richards and Rodgers, 1982), and said that the very concept of method is not helpful (Pennycook, 1989; Prabhu, 1990), but teachers go on believing that if they can just find the right method, all of their students will learn everything they teach. Colleges of education reinforce that belief by requiring that preservice teachers take methods courses, in which they are supposed to learn how to teach. Publishers further reinforce it by publishing methods books for use in those courses, and to enable in-service teachers to remain up-to-date on the latest methods.

It is very unlikely that any teacher would ever be able to implement a "name" method in a classroom in exactly the way it was meant to be done. Even methods that are meant to be "teacher-proof" end up with wide variations in practice. One of the dangers of the very concept of method is precisely that: when methods are implemented in different ways, the results can differ widely. Many promising classroom procedures have earned bad reputations because teachers implement them inappropriately. Methods themselves therefore cannot be adopted ready-made; each teacher must adapt the method to her own style and circumstances.

Even techniques, which are the activities through which a method is implemented, are not transferable without an understanding of the beliefs on which the method and the techniques are based. For example, a technique such as a language experience story uses a student's own language as reading material. The assumption is that if the students read material that they have just spoken it will be familiar to them, which will facilitate the process of learning relationships between sounds and letters. However, if the teachers correct the children's grammar mistakes, writing something that differs from what the children said, the children may make incorrect assumptions about these relationships. If the teachers do not let the children see what they are writing as it is being written, they lose the opportunity to reinforce these relationships. A simple technique can thus lose its effectiveness if it is implemented in ways that do not reflect the beliefs on which it is based.

If methods cannot be transferred from one classroom to another because of differing situations, and techniques cannot be transferred unless the beliefs on which they are based are understood, then teachers' beliefs become very important. All teachers have implicit beliefs that form a theory about how children learn. That theory is implied in everything the teachers do, although they are often not aware of it because they have not consciously thought it out. But the theory still guides them as they choose which activities to do and how to do them. Teachers are often suspicious of theory, however, regarding it as useless, a waste of time, and possibly even dangerous. They want to know what they can do in the classroom tomorrow to make their jobs a little easier. Thinking out their theories and making them explicit could help them much more than learning a lot of new techniques because it is the theories that provide an underlying unity to everything that happens in a classroom, ensuring that techniques work together toward the teacher's goals.

There are two methods that have had a profound influence on my teaching because they helped me to examine my own theories of learning in light of the theories on which the methods were based. Although both include techniques that I have found usable, I could never teach in the same ways that Sylvia Ashton-Warner or Paulo Freire did. Nevertheless, they have both been major influences on my life as a teacher.

In *Teacher* (1963) Sylvia Ashton-Warner describes her experiences teaching five- and six-year-old Maori children in New Zealand. The only materials that were available to teach reading were American **pre-primers**, descendants of *Dick and Jane* called *Janet and John*. The books were based on a sight-word approach with vocabulary that was controlled, limited, and totally uninteresting. One child had spent four months learning three words. With Ashton-Warner's Key Vocabulary (**Key Word**) technique, it took the student only four minutes to learn each word he had chosen. These were "organic" words, important to him because they were associated with his deepest loves and fears. Every day each child chose a word that was important to him or her and the teacher wrote it on a card. The expectation was that these words would become "instant recognition" words because of their importance, and if the next day a child couldn't recognize a word, it was thrown out because it wasn't important.

Mornings in Ashton-Warner's classroom were dedicated to Organic Work. The children used their Key Vocabulary for Creative Writing, and used what they had written for Organic Reading. They also talked and quarreled; danced and sang; worked with water, sand, clay, paint; cried and daydreamed; loved. "Breathing Out" was the creative work; "Breathing In" was intake, reading their own writing, reading each other's writing, being read to. In the afternoon they did "Standard Work," although not in a standard way. "Breathing Out" in the afternoon was the "Golden Section," number study and nature study together, outside. The afternoon's "Breathing In" was "standard" vocabulary, reading of the Maori transitional readers that Ashton-Warner wrote to reflect the children's experiences, and, eventually, reading of the standard *Janet and John* readers.

At the time I read *Teacher*, I was teaching eight- and nine-year-old Hispanic children, and the only materials that were available to teach reading in English were further descendants of *Dick and Jane* called *Janet and Mark*. As I was rebelling against the senselessness of these materials, I read about Ashton-Warner's Organic Reading. As I was struggling with ways of integrating the discrete pieces of the mandated curriculum and trying to find a routine that would work for me, I read about her Daily Rhythm. As I was trying to find ways to make the sterile culture of the school and school materials relevant to my Hispanic children, I read about her Transitional Readers. As I was losing the battle with children who were totally resistant to writing anything, I read about her Organic Writing. As I was trying to find a way to make mathematics meaningful, I read about the Golden Section. As I was hopelessly trying to create an atmosphere of calm out of the chaos in my classroom, I read about Tone.

Of course, reading *Teacher* did not solve all my problems, although Key Vocabulary has become a valuable technique for me, modified each time I use it in a different situation. What worked for Ashton-Warner did not necessarily work for me. For one thing, I needed more structure than Ashton-Warner. What has stayed with me ever since, however, has been a firm belief in the importance of basing any method on the needs of the particular children being taught. When Ashton-Warner's students needed meaningful words to learn as first words, they got their own most significant words to learn. When they had difficulty reading from standard pre-primers, they learned to read by reading their own writing. When they needed real things to make numbers meaningful, they learned about nature and numbers together. When they needed to release excess energy, they talked and danced and created.

Another aspect of Ashton-Warner's method that has become important to me is that because it was organic, it was necessarily integrated. This fit into my growing belief that separating "reading" and "language arts," for example, is ridiculous. How can "spelling" be taught apart from "composition"? With Ashton-Warner's method, all of the children's work developed from them; you cannot do that and at the same time divide the work into reading, writing, language arts, mathematics, science, art, music. For a young child, all are inseparable parts of life. Dividing them up is simply another way of making them into non-sense.

Paulo Freire's method of teaching reading to illiterate adults through "conscientization" (Freire, 1973; Brown, 1978) has been equally important in forming my thinking. I first read about Freire shortly after I had read *Teacher*. There are similarities in the methodologies of both Freire and Ashton-Warner. Both began with words that were deeply meaningful to the learners. Both rejected published primers as beginning reading materials: Ashton-Warner because they were totally irrelevant to her students' lives and the vocabulary was so sterile that her children couldn't learn it, and Freire because he believed that the top-down presentation of text to the learner made the learner an Object of his or her own learning, when what was necessary was an inside-out process in which the learner was Subject. There are similarities in rationale—both built on the learner's sociocultural reality to gain access to standard print. Freire worked with illiterate adults in Brazil forming "culture circles" that tried to eliminate the power differential between "teacher" and "student" by creating dialogue between coordinator and participants. Before any instruction in print conventions occurs, participants talk about the distinction between culture and nature and come to see that all people create culture, and that literacy can open the door to areas of culture previously closed to them.

The mechanics of teaching the **sound-symbol correspondences** in Freire's method are deceptively simple. A list of 16 to 18 "generative" words is developed, different for each locality where culture circles are held. The words are chosen for their high emotional impact on the participants who use them and for their phonetic properties so that they represent all the sound-symbol correspondences of Portuguese. Each word is "codified" by preparing an illustration that stimulates discussion. After the discussion, participants are shown the word, which is then broken into syllables. The initial consonant from each syllable is then paired with each of the five vowels. Learners who can read the initial syllable of the word *tijolo* (brick) are shown how the *ti* changes to *ta, te, to,* or *tu,* depending on which vowel is used. The same is done with *jo,* which becomes *ja, je, ji,* or *ju* as the vowels change. From a three-syllable word, there are fifteen possible consonant/vowel combinations, which are shown on a "discovery card." From these fifteen syllables the learners choose combinations that form other words they know. This process is repeated for each of the "generative" words, and the learners thus learn to read and write all of the sounds of their language. Participants in culture circles come to understand the value of literacy through the "conscientization" process, and most of them master all of the sound-symbol correspondences of Portuguese in approximately 30 to 40 hours of "instruction."

### "Discovery Card" for the word *tijolo* (brick)

| ti | jo | lo |
|----|----|----|
| ta | ja | la |
| te | je | le |
| ti | ji | li |
| to | jo | lo |
| tu | ju | lu |

I learned a lesson about the nontransferability of methods when I tried to use Freire's "discovery card" in my classroom. Because Spanish has the same syllable structure as Portuguese, it was easy to transfer the technique to learning to read in Spanish. I tried to use words that I thought would be meaningful for my students, but I did not use the "conscientization" process. The children enjoyed the "game," and it probably increased their fluency in decoding slightly, but it did little for overall reading ability. I later realized that the essence of Freire's method is not the mechanics of creating new words from syllables. In itself, that is a discrete skill that has little to do with proficient reading. Indeed, it was reminiscent of the syllabic *ma, me, mi, mo, mu* method my students had been subjected to for two years before they came to me, which had produced proficient word callers who understood nothing of what they read. The essence of Freire's method was the conscientization process, which I had shied away from as being too "political." The process in itself, however, is nonpolitical. It only becomes political when its success creates people who can change the political agenda of those in power by demanding their rights. What Freire's conscientization process did was show his learners that they could change their lives. Once they believed this they had a reason to learn to read and write.

If I wanted to "apply" Freire to my teaching situation I had to use his philosophy and beliefs, not necessarily his techniques. I had to find ways to give my students reasons to learn to read and write. In their previous schooling they had come to see reading and writing as nonsensical and unpleasant because it was done without any attention to meaning, and because they had not been able to succeed at it. I needed some kind of a "conscientization" process for my students that would enable them to see reading and writing as both necessary and enjoyable. That was a more difficult task than implementing a technique, but it was the only way "applying" Freire to my situation made any sense.

These two methods worked because they were based on the needs of the learners for whom they were designed. They also worked because the people implementing them believed in the methods and believed in the ability of the learners to succeed using these methods. The best of methods will not work if the teacher using it does not believe in it. For this reason, no methodology can be "imposed" on teachers who do not believe in it. There is a danger that the whole language movement will be distorted as teachers who don't fully understand the approach implement it in ways that contradict its foundations, and as teachers are required to implement whole language techniques when they don't really believe in the approach. Perhaps one of the reasons that **critical pedagogy**, which is based on Freire's beliefs, has been successful whenever it is implemented is that it has not become "popular" and therefore is usually only implemented by people who truly understand it and believe in it.

Case Study, p. 116.

In addition to believing in the method, teachers must believe that the learners will succeed using the method. The power of teacher expectations has been well known for years—children whose teachers expect them to learn do learn, and children whose teachers expect them not to learn do not learn. However, many teachers believe that the power of low expectations does not apply when those expectations are based on their knowledge of the children. They believe that their low expectations are justified because the children are, in fact, functioning at a low level. Carrasco (1981) reports on a study in which videotaped evidence of a bilingual kindergarten girl's behavior in the classroom helped the teacher revise her assessment of the child. The teacher admitted that she had "written her off" (p. 153) on the basis of a kindergarten placement test and her demonstrated lack of the skills required for success in first grade. The teacher had decided midway through the year that there was little likelihood that the child would catch up by the end of the year, so she planned to have her repeat kindergarten. She then stopped calling on that student so as not to embarrass her if she couldn't answer the question or do the task appropriately. The videotapes, however, clearly showed the child acting as both teacher and leader among a group of children working on puzzles during their free time. Thus, the teacher's concern for the child's feelings led to a situation in which the child was not able to demonstrate what she could do, and it was only by chance that the teacher was made aware of her true capabilities.

Teachers may expect less of a student for many reasons. As in the case above, it may be that the teacher believes a child just isn't ready, or she may believe that the child lacks innate ability. Many teachers of bilingual children believe that students can't do cognitively demanding work in a second language; bilingual teachers sometimes also believe that their students can't do that kind of work even in their first language because it is not well developed. These teachers then "water down" the tasks they ask their students to do. The result is that neither the language nor the cognitive ability develops as it should. Lowered expectations, no matter what they are based on, always lead to lowered performance.

It is essential that teachers become aware of their beliefs in many areas. They must believe in the methods they use, but they must also understand why they believe in them. They must believe in themselves, and in their own ability to implement the methods they use. Most importantly, they must believe in the children they teach.

*Does Matilde's implied theory of learning coincide with her description of herself as a whole language teacher? Why or why not?*

*Give examples of times when Matilde demonstrates high expectations for her students and other examples that show low expectations. What evidence is there that students do or do not live up to Matilde's expectations?*

Classroom Research, p. 117.

Reflection

Reflection

## Suggested Readings:

*Key Works:* Ashton-Warner (1963) and Freire (Brown, 1978; Freire, 1973) are "must reading" for teachers of culturally and linguistically different children. Ashton-Warner describes her experiences as a British teacher of Maori children in New Zealand. Brown and Freire describe the process developed by Freire to teach the fundamentals of literacy in Portuguese to illiterate Brazilian peasants. Both Ashton-Warner and Freire demonstrate the power of methods in which teachers believe.

Collins and Tamarkin (1990) give a vivid description of the power of teacher expectations. Marva Collins believed in her poor, black, undereducated students, and the stories she tells of their achievement are inspirational. Mike Rose (1995) also presents vivid portraits of teachers who make public education work because they believe in the children they teach. Rose visited successful urban and rural schools and classrooms across the country; he describes the programs, their contexts, and the issues confronting teachers, students, and administrators. Many of the classrooms he includes serve bilingual children, and one chapter deals specifically with bilingual education.

## Children learn when they are involved
## in determining what and how they will learn

Journal

On pp. 43-44, Matilde explains how she planned the Native American unit described on pp. 36-37.

*Think about different ways in which teachers you know do their planning. What relationship might there be between methods of planning and teachers' personalities, teaching styles, or theories of learning? What implications might this have for your own planning?*

Most teachers have been taught that they must carefully preplan their lessons so they will know exactly what they're going to do when they go into the classroom each day. For beginning teachers those well-developed plans provide security that they are teaching effectively. For more experienced teachers, plans that were carefully prepared in the past can mean they don't have to work so hard on planning in the present. Teachers who spend innumerable hours developing a particular unit assume that they will be able to use the fruits of their labors for many years to come. But how can lessons that were developed for use with one class meet the needs of another? How can teachers decide by themselves what will interest and engage their students? Don't students need to be involved in the planning of their own learning?

Interest and engagement are not the only reasons for involving students in the planning of their own learning. Teachers who consistently tell students what to do and how to do it run the risk that their students will become dependent on the teacher, do only what they're told to do, and never develop the ability to plan and carry out any kind of learning on their own. Teachers who share the planning process with their students help their students to realize that they are responsible for their own learning.

Connie White's (1991) poignant monograph, *Jevon Doesn't Sit at the Back Anymore*, highlights the importance of including children in the planning process. It is a moving example of how one classroom teacher implemented **action research** in her classroom and the benefits that accrued from the self-observation and assessment that go with researching one's own teaching. White describes how her teaching changed through her efforts to reach a child named Jevon, who was spending his second year with her in kindergarten. As she describes her previous approach, it appears a model of **whole language** teaching, with reading taught through chants, poems, songs, stories, and **big books**. Writing was taught through journals and group and individual writing projects, with a lot of modeling and conferencing. There was a story time each day, and activities were connected through themes. But, as White says, "*I* decided the theme areas and topics, *I* decided the activities, *I* directed the learning. That first year I taught Jevon he didn't learn much in school" (p. 5).

The following year White decided to observe Jevon, collecting data on what he did and didn't do, and on what seemed to interest him. She found that his interest in and knowledge of farms and farm life were not reflected in her chosen themes, so he had no voice in the classroom. As she explains, "By the very nature of my teaching practice, which had me direct all activities, I'd shut out Jevon's voice and not allowed his language to be whole in my classroom" (p. 30).

As White watched Jevon, she began to discover how he learned. She found that he could read the names of all the other students in the class, and capitalized on this to bring meaning to her instruction of letters and sounds. She learned to follow his lead when he showed interest in something and to not shut him out by responding too quickly to topics initiated by other students. Jevon finally suggested a book about a horse for story time. When she read it, he sat down right next to her to listen and contributed his comments toward creating its meaning. A borrowed book about a dead cow elicited even more comments, and from then on, Jevon always sat in the front during story time.

Connie White's students now have choices, based on their own interests. More and more teachers are realizing that it is not enough to link various activities together through themes they presume the children are interested in. The children must have a part in the selection of the themes and in planning how to implement them.

I learned about one way to do this the first time I went to a workshop presented by Barbara Flores and her colleagues (Castro et al., 1986). Flores has worked for many years with bilingual teachers in Arizona and California, helping them to institute whole language techniques in their classrooms and to use action research to study their own teaching. At the workshop, a first-grade teacher described how, on the first day of school, she simply asked the children what they wanted to learn. Although they sometimes needed a little prompting to think beyond learning to read and write, the teacher soon got them talking about dolphins, bones, caterpillars, and stars. The suggested topics were written on a chart, and the children voted on which one they wanted to begin with. They then brainstormed everything they already knew about the topic, and what they wanted to learn, with the teacher writing it all down on charts. Planning for the learning process was done collaboratively. The teacher had to suggest some activities at first, but as the children became accustomed to this way of learning, they began to suggest activities themselves. Both teacher and students worked on collecting all the materials they could find about the chosen topic, and groups were set up to do the various tasks. As information was gathered by each group it was shared with the rest of the class through stories, charts, pictures, murals, and other projects.

Over the next few years, Flores and her colleagues (Edelsky et al., 1991; Garcia et al., 1989; Romero et al., 1987) developed this model of thematic teaching into what they call **theme cycles**. A topic is negotiated and the knowledge the students already have about the topic is recorded. Learning activities are planned collaboratively and materials are collected. Students carry out their planned activities and present what they have learned to the rest of the class. The class returns to the original brainstorming charts to check the accuracy of their previous knowledge, to answer the questions they had framed, and to develop new questions. From this process, a new topic emerges and the cycle begins anew.

Whitmore and Crowell (1994) have written a vivid description of how children invent their own curriculum through theme cycles. Crowell is the teacher of a third-grade bilingual classroom in Arizona, and Whitmore is a researcher who spent two years in that classroom as a participant-observer. Their descriptions provide rich detail on the mechanics of implementing theme cycles, as well

**Investigations**

Prepare a list of counter-arguments to the position that children must be involved in planning their own learning.

as the effects of involving children in planning their own learning and the benefits of sharing classroom power with them.

Theme cycles differ from **thematic units** which are usually planned in advance, meaning that the teacher makes decisions about what will be learned and how. Theme cycles allow children to be active participants in the development of their curriculum. Their needs, interests, and curiosities are incorporated into the planning process. White provides a strong rationale for including children in the planning process: "I don't want to miss what the children need to know the most by planning their curriculum without them" (1990, p. 37).

Theme cycles also differ from thematic units in that thematic units use topics or themes as a means of teaching other subjects or skills, whereas theme cycles use subjects to investigate topics or themes (Edelsky et al., 1991). The difference is that in theme cycles the content is treated seriously in and of itself. Edelsky has commented that thematic teaching must be more than simply "glue to hold separate school subjects together" (1991, p. 165). We learn about topics because they are interesting and valuable in and of themselves, not because they can help us learn something else. Science should be practiced as scientists do, not as science activities tacked on to a unit about cowboys.

It is also important that the content children learn about be related to their lives in authentic ways. There is a growing call to go beyond whole language to critical approaches. Walsh (1993) gave a clear description of traditional, holistic, and critical approaches to learning. She shows how the approaches differ in their concepts of what knowledge is, how it is acquired, and the role of the learners' experience. Traditional approaches consider knowledge a neutral universal entity, a quantifiable and verifiable series of facts. These facts are unrelated to students' previous experiences, and they can be transmitted to students in a systematic way. Whole language approaches view knowledge as the interaction of prior knowledge and experience with new knowledge and experience. Knowledge is acquired through holistic, authentic use, so learning is an active, student-centered process in which all students' experiences are equally valued and built on. Critical approaches see knowledge as partial and problematic because it is always bound to particular conditions. Knowledge is acquired through reflection and action (Walsh, 1991, uses the term *praxis* for this combination of reflection and action as a means of transforming reality) and is grounded in experience that is shaped by the power relations of a particular situation. Although **critical pedagogy** is not a methodology with a set of established procedures, Walsh lists several common elements found in critical classrooms, including a belief in the participatory nature of learning, the use of dialogue to foster open exchange, redirection of the curriculum based on generative problem-themes, and incorporation of both reflection and action (1993, pp. 55-56).

In critical approaches, themes come from issues in which students want to be involved, issues that have real-life purposes. Problem-posing techniques are used so themes from the students' own lives become the basis of dialogue and critical thinking, and reflection on these themes becomes action (Wallerstein, 1987). In this way, the content of the classroom is connected to the students, their communities, and their society. These techniques provide a means for students to have an impact on the environment. Peterson (1991) gives a moving account of

Case Study,
p. 117.

Critical
perspectives
are described
in more detail
in Learn
by Doing
on pp. 74-75
and 77-78.

Classroom
Research
p. 117.

how a fifth-grade bilingual teacher uses a critical approach to teach organically, empower his students, implement a dialogical instructional method, and critique the curriculum and society.

Critical approaches provide one way of ensuring that students are involved in planning their own learning; theme cycles and other means of jointly planning the curriculum are other ways in which this can be done. Because student involvement ensures that students are interested in what they are learning, it is an effective way of banishing nonsense from the classroom and helping students to make connections between what they do in school and their experiences outside school, thereby giving all students a more equal chance at success.

*Think of ways in which Matilde could involve her students more in planning their own learning. Which of these could be implemented with very little change in procedures, and which would involve major changes?*

Peterson's approach is described more fully in Learn by Doing on p. 75.

Reflection

## Suggested Readings:

*Key Works:* My views on planning have been influenced by accounts of other teachers' planning processes. Connie White's (1990) account of her discovery of the importance of involving students in their own planning is a moving and memorable monograph. Most of my own knowledge of how to use theme cycles in planning came from attending workshops presented by teachers who were using them, but Edelsky, Altwerger, and Flores (1991) provide a description of theme cycles and how they differ from thematic units.

Two books describe real classrooms in which students create the curriculum: Whitmore and Crowell (1994) report on a two-year ethnographic study of a bilingual classroom, cowritten by the researcher and the teacher. There are detailed descriptions of how the children negotiate the curriculum for the year and create a theme cycle about the Middle Ages. Levy (1996) gives a personal account of one teacher's beliefs, including detailed descriptions of projects that developed from students' questions.

## Children learn when they have control
## over the technology used to help them learn

Journal

A description of how Matilde's students use computers is on pp. 44-46.

Smith's book *Insult to Intelligence* introduces and explains the r-bbit; it is discussed in more detail in *Authentic Purpose* on p. 70.

*List all the uses you can think of for computers in a bilingual classroom. Then arrange them on a continuum from most to least beneficial for the students, explaining why you placed each where you did.*

A few years ago the debate about computers in schools centered on whether they should be used. The question is no longer *whether* to use them, but *how*. Computers are here, in computer labs and in classrooms, and they are here to stay. They have the potential to control the way teachers teach and learners learn, in much the same way that programmatic basal reading materials can control instruction in reading (Smith, 1986). They also have the potential to liberate classrooms from the limitations imposed by isolation in space and time by providing worldwide instantaneous interactive communication.

Frank Smith (1986) calls computers the natural habitat of the r-bbit. The r-bbit is his symbol for the kind of instruction that assumes that children learn through multiple-choice or fill-in-the-blank exercises that present isolated bits of information in small doses. If instruction is a matter of breaking down knowledge into component discrete skills, presenting these skills one at a time in sequential fashion, testing them to be sure they have been acquired, giving extra practice to students who have not mastered them, and continuing the practice/retest cycle until "mastery" has been achieved, then using computers for instruction is eminently logical. Computers can easily keep track of where each student is in the skills sequence and automatically begin each session precisely where the last one ended. They can untiringly provide immediate feedback about whether the student is right or wrong on each practice exercise. They can automatically provide extra practice for those who need it. They can quickly print out all the information any teacher or administrator might need about which skills each student has mastered. For those who believe that this kind of mastery learning is the key to improving education, this is an appealing scenario. For those who believe, as Frank Smith and I do, that this kind of "learning" bears no relationship at all to the ways in which children learn naturally and leads to dependence, loss of true reading and writing skills, and inability to think critically, it is a nightmare to be avoided at all costs.

The question of how computers are used is particularly important for teachers working with students who have been judged "at risk." The commonly accepted solution to their "problems," that of giving them massive doses of **basic skills**, is something that computers can provide in a very efficient way. While these students are being drilled by computers on discrete skills that bear no resemblance to what people actually do when they read and write, their more privileged peers will be using computers as tools to help them solve real-world problems. In addition, if the "at-risk" students don't speak English, they will be limited to using computer programs that involve very little language, which eliminates many of the more creative programs available.

On the other hand, educators who believe that classroom interactions should be based on real communication and authentic tasks see technology as a tool that can help provide that authenticity. They reject the image of the computer as a tutor that provides instruction and practice and instead see it as a tool that helps students perform interesting, creative, and important tasks. In this view, computers are used in much the same ways that they are used outside the classroom.

One of the most common uses of computers as a tool, both within and outside schools, is as word processors. Word processing programs are especially suitable for use in bilingual classes, since no special program is needed for students who write in languages other than English. Most word processing programs can print accents and other special characters, and fonts are available for non-Roman alphabets.

As even prolific writers will attest, it is much easier to "put bad words on paper," an essential step in writing a first draft, when the writer knows that they can be changed without leaving a trace. (I heard this phrase in a radio interview years ago. Its impact on me has been great; I could not have written this book without first putting a lot of very bad words on paper.) The ease with which text can be deleted, inserted, and moved inspires confidence in even the most timid writer. Brisk (1985) provides an example of how computer use can facilitate writing. She studied the writing of a group of first-grade bilingual students in the classroom and in the computer room. Children who wrote only single sentences in the classroom, and then only with great difficulty, wrote multisentence stories in the computer room.

However, simply using a computer to write meaningless sentences for a nonexistent audience will not tap into the computer's potential to facilitate writing. There must be a reason for writing, a reason that goes beyond writing just because the teacher told you to. In Brisk's study it was not only the use of the computer to facilitate writing and revising that affected the children's writing. In the computer room the children talked about what they wanted to write before they began writing. The stories they wrote were printed out, illustrated, and bound into books. Any spelling or punctuation errors were corrected by the teachers, without comment, before each story was printed. However, if the children asked questions about spelling and punctuation while they were writing, these questions were answered (MacGowan, 1986).

Using computers to create books, or any other form of writing, remains somewhat artificial, however, without an authentic audience outside the students' own classroom. Telecommunications is the perfect tool to provide the authenticity that is so difficult to create when tasks are limited to the confines of the four walls of a classroom. Telecommunications can provide a distant audience without the delays that make mail exchanges less than satisfactory. The near-instantaneous nature of the communication keeps motivation at a very high level.

Dennis Sayers has written a great deal about computer networking for bilingual students (Cummins and Sayers, 1995; Sayers, 1986, 1993; Sayers and Brown, 1987). Long before most people had ever heard of the **Internet,** he and Cynthia Brown had established a computer network, *De orilla a orilla* (From Shore to Shore), *Orillas* for short, that linked bilingual classes in Hartford and San Diego with **"sister classes"** in Puerto Rico and Mexico. Sayers recognized the potential of telecommunications from the beginning. A distant class would provide a perfect audience for presentation of one's work or, better yet, for collaboration on the work itself. The kind of negotiation of meaning that would have to occur through writing as students investigate different aspects of a problem and share their findings would be similar to what Shirley Brice Heath did when she made students into her research assistants (Heath, 1985). Using literacy to find out what you know helps move that literacy to higher levels.

Heath's project is described in more detail in Authentic Purpose on pp. 69-70.

Another inspirational aspect of telecommunications is its natural tie-in to dialogue journals. **Dialogue journals** provide a strong motivation to write because the writer always knows that he or she will get an immediate answer. This contrasts with pen pals or any other form of letter writing, in which you never know when—or if—you will get an answer. With computer networks, dialogue journals can be exchanged with partners any place in the world.

In addition to improving writing, another goal of the *Orillas* network is to foster self-esteem. Paired classes communicate through the network, exchanging cultural packages, producing joint newspapers, and conducting shared investigations (Sayers, 1993; Sayers and Brown, 1987). As bilingual students in the United States recognize that there are students in other places for whom Spanish (or whatever other language the students are bilingual in) is the natural, only, and accepted form of communication in school, they come to realize that their first language is not inferior, nor is it a language they should forget as they learn English.

One of the projects done over the *Orillas* network is described by Brown (1993). Students collected more than 600 proverbs, which were published and sent to all participating classes. Different classes then won prizes for having the most of a particular kind of proverb. Students made drawings of proverbs, wrote fables illustrating the proverbs, collected contradictory proverbs, and wrote essays on "What's Wrong with This Proverb." Other network projects include a survey of endangered species, an international human rights project, and an intergenerational investigation of childhood games.

Telecommunications Project, p. 117.

With the Internet becoming increasingly accessible to schools, projects of this kind become easier to undertake. Innumerable discussion groups and bulletin boards are dedicated to elementary school telecommunications projects. For example, one children's network posts monthly problems involving mathematics. Students post their answers to the problem along with an explanation of how they solved the problem. Multisite science projects can have students all over the world recording weather patterns or collecting data about air and water pollution. Easy-to-use bulletin boards facilitate matching classes anywhere in the world for any kind of project.

Case Study, p. 118.

There are many other ways in which technology can be used as a tool. Pease-Alvarez and Vásquez (1990) report on a cross-age tutoring program in which sixth-grade Latina girls tutored Spanish-speaking second and third graders in computer use. Students who spoke very little in normal classroom interaction became articulate in tutoring sessions, and students took responsibility for the tutoring themselves, with teachers serving only as facilitators. Peyton and Batson (1986) describe how a classroom full of computers linked through a local area network enabled deaf students to be immersed in English and thus develop their English writing skills. Peyton and Batson also discuss the application of this technology to other language-learning situations. DeVillar and Faltis

(1991) and González-Edfelt (1990) advocate the use of computers in conjunction with **cooperative learning** to help integrate culturally heterogeneous classrooms and thus facilitate language learning by linguistic minorities.

What all these examples have in common is their use of technology as a tool to do something real, something interesting, something creative. Technology used in this way can be a means of creating communities among linguistic minority students and of fostering pride in bilingual students' native languages and cultures. In addition, learners have control over the technology and over their own learning. This is important not only for the empowerment of students and for their independence as learners but also, as Frank Smith explains, "because in the conflict between teachers and r-bbits, the side that controls the computers will be the victors" (1986, p. 203).

*What do you think would be the most effective use of the computer equipment in Matilde's classroom (three Apple computers, word processing software, reading and math software, and a modem and phone line)?*

Classroom
Research,
p 118.

Reflection

## *Suggested Readings:*

*Key Works:* I learned about the potential of telecommunications and technology in bilingual education in workshops, but two recent articles summarize much of the early work that was done in this area. Brown (1993) recounts three projects in which technology is used in humanistic ways to create community, and Sayers (1993) gives examples of how telecommunications has been used to develop native and second language literacy.

Faltis and DeVillar (1990) edited a special issue of the journal Computers in the Schools dedicated to language minority students and computers. Although technology has advanced immensely since the issue's publication, the ideas for collaborative use of computers and other technology are still valid. DeVillar and Faltis (1991) combine principles of communication, integration, and cooperation with computer-integrated instruction to provide a plan for incorporating computer use into heterogeneous classrooms in ways that will make school experiences more positive for all racial and ethnic groups.

Cummins and Sayers (1995) have written three books in one: moving examples of ways in which telecommunications can promote cultural understanding and literacy; a powerful theoretical challenge to those who advocate basic skills and cultural literacy; a comprehensive list of Internet resources that relate to bilingual education and to education in general, and instructions for using telecommunications.

## The amount of use of each language, and the ways in which each is used, should be consciously determined

Journal

Examples of ways in which Spanish and English are used in Matilde's classroom are found on pp. 46-49.

*Think about how bilingual teachers you have observed or worked with use their two languages in the classroom. Do they keep them separate or mix them? Do they use them in equal or unequal amounts? Record your thoughts about how the two languages should be used.*

The success of a particular **bilingual education** program model may depend on decisions individual teachers make about which language to use when. Unfortunately, these decisions are often not conscious. Language use in a bilingual classroom is frequently a reflection of the relative language proficiency of the teacher; nonfluent bilinguals have a tendency to favor their stronger language, whereas fluent bilinguals are often unaware of which language they are speaking. The consistent use of one language more than the other may also be a subconscious reflection of the teacher's assimilationist or separatist views. Teachers with little background in bilingual methodology may not even be aware that language use is an issue. Often teachers believe that they are using both languages equally when, in fact, the sociolinguistic forces in favor of English allow English to encroach on the native language to a great extent.

The debate over language use has traditionally been couched in terms of decisions about whether to maintain a complete separation of languages or allow concurrent use. If languages are to be separated, questions arise about which languages to use with which subjects, at which times, or with which people. If languages are to be used concurrently, the questions concern how to implement this strategy in a principled way, or whether simply to allow the natural **codeswitching** that occurs in bilingual communities. It has generally been assumed that language arts instruction would normally be done monolingually in each language, so that the question of language use has been focused on content areas and noninstructional language use. Increased interest in the use of the native language to facilitate acquisition and development of the second language makes this division problematic, however, and the integration of language and content teaching also makes it increasingly difficult to speak about either one alone. Therefore, the question of language use is no longer as simple as deciding which language to use in teaching a particular subject, or which time of day to use each language.

I spent much of my bilingual teaching career trying to find a solution to the problem of how to use the two languages in my classroom. If I did not monitor my language use, I found that I used English almost exclusively, using Spanish only for Spanish reading instruction and with those children who did not understand English. My students followed my lead, using more and more English. When I realized what was happening I decided to implement a system of language separation because I believed in **additive bilingualism** and did not want my students to accept the idea that acquiring English meant forgetting Spanish, or that learning could only be done in English.

My experiments with language separation were interesting, if not always successful. I found that trying to keep languages separate entailed an almost-constant battle against the natural inclination of fluent bilinguals to codeswitch. However, I did settle into a fairly comfortable pattern of predominant use of one language in the morning and of the other in the afternoon.

My interest in the question of separation of languages in bilingual classrooms has continued, and my opinions have changed as I have become more familiar with different contexts of classroom language use. I have observed **whole language** bilingual classrooms in the Northeast, where mixed language use often leads to a very strong preference for English and the loss of Spanish skills, and I have learned about whole language bilingual classrooms in the Southwest, where mixed language use often leads to natural development of oral and written skills in both languages. I have seen English-speaking children become fluent in French in immersion programs in which the languages are totally separated, and I have seen them become fluent, or not become fluent, in Spanish in two-way bilingual programs in which language separation is not as strictly enforced. It is difficult to arrive at any kind of generalization about appropriate language use.

What I am therefore going to do in this section is present both sides of the debate over keeping languages separate in a bilingual program. I will follow this with a compromise position that I believe preserves the best features of both sides, but readers must recognize that individual decisions have to be made on the basis of particular contexts.

For more than two decades proponents of bilingual education have been advocating separation of languages in bilingual programs. From the earliest *Handbook of Bilingual Education* (Saville and Troike, 1971), to the recent *Bilingual Education Handbook* (Bilingual Education Office, State of California, 1990), the recommendation has been that "sticking with [one language] for sustained periods without translation or recourse to the alternative language appears to be superior to a mixed-language approach" (Bilingual Education Office, State of California, 1990, p. 43). The arguments given for this separation of languages include factors related to bilingual language acquisition, second language acquisition, and sociolinguistics.

The argument from bilingual language acquisition is that children who are exposed to mixed language input develop a mixed code. If they never hear either language used separately from the other they will not develop the ability to use one language without mixing it with the other. If we want students who can function in each language monolingually, without interference from one to the other, the languages should be kept separate in the input.

The argument from second language acquisition applies to children who enter a bilingual program with little or no proficiency in one of the two languages. When languages are not separated, children quickly learn that if they don't understand something in one language, it will be repeated in the other. Trying to understand complex content in the weaker language is difficult work that children will avoid if they can. They therefore tune out the input in their weaker language because it is not necessary for them to understand. Input that is tuned out does not become intake, and therefore cannot contribute to language acquisition. If children are proficient enough in both languages so they don't need to tune out the weaker language during concurrent language use, they will soon get bored by hearing everything twice.

The argument from sociolinguistics is that unless language use is controlled, the language that dominates in society will dominate in the classroom. For programs whose goal is to maintain balanced use of both languages, separation of languages may be the only way to accomplish this goal. Legarreta (1977) observed four classrooms in which the official goal was to use each language half the time. Three of the classrooms used a concurrent approach, in which both languages were used interchangeably, while one used an alternate-day approach. The alternate-day classroom was the only one that came close to 50 percent use of the minority language. Although the teachers in the other classes thought they were using Spanish about 50 percent of the time, in actual practice the average amount of Spanish use was 28 percent. Other studies have shown similar results; even in a two-way bilingual program with alternate-day language use and a stated goal of developing bilingualism and biliteracy, McCollum (1994) found that, for academic purposes, the Hispanic students used English almost exclusively. The sociolinguistic hegemony of English in the United States tends to diminish use of the native language.

When and how a bilingual teacher uses each of the two languages in the classroom has a profound effect on the students' views of the importance of those languages. Separation of languages can serve to emphasize the importance of the native language and to mitigate against the influence of English as the "prestige" language. This is particularly important when minority students have developed negative attitudes towards their own language and see English as being more important. In one two-way bilingual program, when it was discovered that even kindergarten students preferred English, one of the steps taken to try to change those attitudes was to "[separate] languages for instruction by alternating days of instruction..., thereby ensuring that Spanish had equal time and status and was used for all academic and literacy learning tasks" (Jones, 1993, p. 237). If bilingualism and biliteracy are truly goals of a bilingual program, it is essential to foster a positive attitude toward the native language. Extra effort must be made to protect the native language from the oppressively strong domination by English. The evidence is overwhelming that when concurrent language use is allowed, English predominates. Many people believe that separation of languages is the only way to protect and conserve the native languages.

The different ways of ensuring the separation of languages in bilingual programs have been summarized by Jacobson (1990). Separation by person requires that a different person speak to the students consistently in each language. This can be done with a team-teaching model, with a teacher and a native language aide, or with a teacher and parent volunteers. However, care should be taken not to send a hidden message about language prestige by having the higher-status teacher always speaking English and the lower-status aide or parent always speaking the minority language (Lessow-Hurley, 1996). Separation by topic means that some subjects are taught in each language. The language in which the subject is taught may vary from year to year, or the same subject may always be taught in the same language. Again, care must be taken to prevent technological subjects such as science and math from being consistently associated with English (Lessow-Hurley, 1996). Separation by time involves alternating years, months, weeks, days, half-days, or class periods. Separation by physical location uses different rooms or different areas of the same room for each language.

Obviously, various combinations of these ways of separating languages are possible. One common model involves all four factors: students spend half the day learning certain subjects with one teacher in his or her room and the other half on other subjects with another teacher in a different room. Another common technique is called Preview/Review. A lesson is introduced in one language, taught in the other, and reviewed in the first. This provides separation of languages if the different parts of the lesson are taught by different people, at different times, or in different places.

In all cases, teachers wishing to separate languages must try to avoid repeating the same lessons in both languages. Repetition is a needless waste of time because it doubles the amount of time needed to teach any particular aspect of the curriculum; it is also boring for students.

In spite of all the arguments advanced by proponents of language separation, if one observes bilingual classrooms of all sorts, the most common way of using the two languages is some kind of concurrent use. Even in programs designed to separate the languages, teachers use both (Faltis, 1990). The reason for this is that separation of languages is not a natural linguistic phenomenon. When two languages coexist in a community, speakers of both languages naturally switch back and forth between them. Codeswitching is not seen by linguists as an imperfect use of both languages, but rather as an enhanced, additional code at the disposal of bilingual speakers (Grosjean, 1982). In bilingual classrooms, any attempt at keeping languages separate must be artificially enforced, and is therefore likely to fail. Concurrent use is a much better reflection of how the community uses language.

In addition to its naturalness, a strong argument for concurrent use of two languages in a bilingual program is that it is the only way to ensure that all students understand everything going on in class. No matter how carefully one structures the language in a second-language content class, some of the content will be lost when learners are not proficient in the language of instruction. The extra cognitive effort required to process complex concepts in a second language puts an additional strain on second language learners. When academic content is the primary goal, there is no reason to prohibit the use of the native language (Milk, 1990). Bilingual education is first and foremost an *educational* program —it is not a program of language teaching. Bilingual students must be assisted in developing sophisticated concepts, mastering complex skills, and completing cognitively demanding tasks. In order to do this, every available resource should be used. The first language of the students is one such resource, and it makes no sense not to use it whenever it can help.

Separation of languages means that the child's native language will be prohibited at certain times, in certain places, or with certain people. One of the goals of bilingual education is to promote self-esteem and a positive attitude toward the native language. Prohibition of the native language makes it impossible for children to express themselves fully, thus contributing toward a poor self-image and creating negative attitudes toward the native language.

There are various ways to implement a concurrent approach to language use.

Case Study,
p. 118.

Two of these could be considered the defaults. In other words, these are the approaches used when a conscious decision has not been made to use something else. They are random switching (there are no apparent patterns or conscious decisions involved in switching from one language to the other), and concurrent translation (everything that is said in one language is repeated in the other). Random switching might be considered the most natural pattern of dual language use and concurrent translation the most effective in ensuring that everything is understood.

A new approach to concurrent language use has been developed by Jacobson (1981, 1990). This approach uses switching strategies that are present in the community, provides for an equal amount of use of both languages, and ensures that the teaching of content is not interrupted. Switches are made only in response to identified cues, and they must also be related to a specific learning objective. Teachers wishing to use this program are trained to recognize and make decisions about these cues.

Whatever approach is taken to concurrent language use in the classroom, it is generally accepted that it will be more effective if repetition and immediate translation are avoided. A language switch should serve to reinforce and expand what was said in the other language, not repeat it.

**Investigations**

Organize a debate around the proposition that languages should be totally separated in a bilingual program.

Clearly there are compelling arguments on both sides of this issue. If we look to classroom-based empirical research to help solve the argument we find contradictory evidence. One study found that effective teachers use whatever language is necessary to ensure student understanding. Tikunoff and Vázquez-Faria (1982) reported on an observational study of 58 teachers who had been nominated by their peers and administrators as effective bilingual teachers. One of the things these effective teachers did was to mediate instruction to ensure that students with limited English proficiency had access to it. They did this by using the native language whenever needed to achieve clarity. Another study, however, found that effective bilingual teachers keep the languages separate. Wong Fillmore (1982) observed four bilingual classrooms and found a great deal of variation in the amount of language learning that occurred in each. One of the factors associated with the best language learning situations was that the teachers kept the two languages separate without translating from one to the other.

In trying to reconcile these two positions I have developed a compromise position that establishes a basic separation of languages, giving approximately equal time to both. This separation can be done by having different teachers for each language, or by using each language at a different time. During the time that the native language is being used, no intrusion from English should be allowed. Since the native language is in danger of being replaced, it needs to be guarded and protected. However, during the time when English is being used, the native language could be used as necessary to facilitate acquisition of English and to ensure comprehension of content. This kind of program could help maintain the importance of the native language in transitional bilingual programs without sacrificing the advantages of codeswitching in certain situations.

Sometimes it is the second language rather than the native language that must be "protected" or it will not be acquired naturally. In situations in which the native language is not in danger of being replaced and the second language would not normally be acquired unless the environment is structured in some way to facilitate it, separation of languages can be used to ensure acquisition of the second language. This is the case with Anglo children learning another language in an immersion or two-way bilingual program or in foreign language classrooms. In these cases, no intrusion from the native language would be allowed.

In both of these cases it is the nonmajority language that will not be acquired (or maintained) unless it is supported and protected by keeping it separate from the majority language. Edelsky (1991, pp. 24–28) has used the linguistic terminology "marked" and "unmarked" to explain this phenomenon. The unmarked language (English, in the case of linguistic minority children in the United States) will normally be acquired by minority students even without any special attention being given to it. It also will not be lost by majority students. It does not need to be protected, and codeswitching during English use can be tolerated; indeed, it can be encouraged whenever it is useful to help achieve understanding. The marked language (Spanish, or any other minority language), will not normally be acquired by majority students unless special attention is given to it. It can also easily be lost by minority students. It should be protected from the incursion of English by not allowing any codeswitching when it is being used.

In all cases, dogmatic prescriptive statements can do more harm than good. Decisions must be made based on the relative statuses of the two languages in the community, the goals of the community regarding language maintenance or language shift, community attitudes toward codeswitching, the goals of the bilingual education program, the academic background and language proficiency of the students, and the teacher's particular teaching style and language proficiency. When programmatic guidelines exist, as in the case of immersion programs or two-way bilingual programs in which separation of languages is part of the model, teachers should of course follow the guidelines. In most cases, however, bilingual teachers find themselves with a class of bilingual students and no guidelines. I can't tell these teachers whether to try to separate languages. I can only tell them that they should weigh all the factors discussed above and then make a decision for themselves.

*Analyze Matilde's use of Spanish and English. What patterns do you see in the choices she makes? How does her actual language use relate to her expressed views on language use, as discussed on pp. 46-47?*

Classroom
Research,
p. 119.

Reflection

## *Suggested Readings:*

*Key Works:* Edelsky's (1991, pp. 24–28) explanation for why second languages are learned in some situations and not in others corresponds with my experience. It also provides more evidence for the fact that marked languages will not be learned unless they are protected. Escamilla (1994) makes the same point in her case study of a bilingual school. Her study focuses on the importance of the context in providing support for minority language use.

Jacobson and Faltis (1990) have collected articles about language distribution issues in bilingual classrooms. Most of the articles, including Jacobson's rationale for the New Concurrent Approach, argue for some variation of mixed language use. A similar approach, which maintains somewhat more separation of languages, is Planned Alternation of Languages (PAL), described by Romero and Parrino (1994).

There are many studies dealing with codeswitching, most of which advocate it as a natural communication method among bilinguals and an appropriate teaching strategy. Huerta-Macías and Quintero (1992) is one such example.

## Children must be assessed in ways that reflect both natural language use and the ways in which they learn

*Record your own experiences with standardized achievement and/or language proficiency testing as a student, a teacher, or an observer. Reflect on your opinions about these and other forms of testing.*

When we want to assess a skill, most of the time we do it by watching a performance of the skill. This is true for such diverse skills as driving a car, typing, or playing the piano. We do not test samples of subskills presumed to make up the skill in question, we do not create artificial simulations of the skill in question. Why is it that when we want to assess people's skill in language, we ask them to do all kinds of tasks that are only remotely related to real language use?

The diversity of tests that are related to bilingual children's use of language is mind-boggling. There are dominance tests, proficiency tests, diagnostic tests, placement tests, achievement tests. Very few of them actually test what they claim to. Very few of them sample language as it is used naturally. When confronted with testing situations, bilingual teachers must be especially sensitive to the presence of nonsense.

Examples of nonsense in testing abound. The very idea that any test can determine **language dominance** is nonsense because language dominance—if such a thing even exists—varies from domain to domain. Many bilingual individuals find it easier to speak one language in a certain situation, easier to speak one language with a certain person, easier to speak one language to talk about a certain topic. An instructional aide with whom I worked for several years could use either English or Spanish with equal ease in school, but when I visited her in her home, she didn't complete a single sentence in English. Home was Spanish. Many bilingual children, even if they are in bilingual classes, associate school with English, which can affect their scores on dominance tests.

Even if the very concept of testing language dominance were not in itself nonsensical, anybody looking at dominance tests objectively would have to be struck by the nonsensical nature of the tasks children are asked to do on those tests. One dominance test actually tests memory, asking the child to repeat mixed sets of Spanish and English words. Another has the child read mixed lists of English and Spanish words where some words, such as "hospital" or "dime" could be read as either English or Spanish. These are tasks that bear very little relationship to what a child's "preferred" or "easier" language might be.

These dominance tests do not claim to measure language ability, only to tell which language is "stronger." Tests of language proficiency do claim to measure ability, and the results of these tests are given in terms of "fluent English speaker," "limited English speaker," or "non-English speaker." Proficiency tests engage children in tasks that seem to be more directly related to language use, but care must be taken to examine exactly what it is that is being tested. One popular proficiency test assesses whether a child can produce correct forms of a

Journal

Testing and assessment practices in Matilde's classroom are described on pp. 50-55.

small set of morphemes. The theory behind this test is that these morphemes are acquired in a particular order; therefore, a child who has acquired only a few of them is at a lower overall proficiency level than one who has acquired more. However, these morphemes are fairly early acquisitions, so although the test may discriminate well at lower levels of language proficiency, it cannot tell whether a student has the ability to deal with the abstract language needed for success in schooling in a second language. With another test, half the final score is based on the retelling of a fanciful story heard on a tape, cued by pictures that are so stylized they can be difficult to interpret. This can penalize children who are not used to hearing or telling fanciful stories, children who cannot interpret stylized drawings, or children who are shy and produce very little language in response to the task.

These tests are so inaccurate in their assessment of language proficiency that one study (Ulibarri, Spencer, and Rivas, 1981) showed that two different tests could be given to the same child on the same day, with one test showing that the child had no English proficiency and the other showing that the child was a fluent English speaker. The child could be placed in a bilingual program and exited from it on the same day if two different tests were used for entry and exit assessment.

Even if language proficiency tests were able to accurately assess bilingual students' abilities in each of their two languages, they would not present a complete picture of a bilingual child's language. This is because bilingual language proficiency is more than the sum of a child's monolingual proficiency in each language. For example, vocabulary tests may show a bilingual child to be below grade level in both languages. However, the words she knows in one language are not necessarily the same words she knows in the other language. If all the words she knew in both languages were combined, the child would probably have a greater total vocabulary than monolingual children of the same age.

In addition to oral proficiency tests, most bilingual programs also give a written test when they are assessing students for exit from the program. In some cases a cloze reading test is given. A **cloze test** is made by taking a reading passage of a particular ability level, deleting every seventh or ninth word from the passage, and asking the students to fill in the correct words. These tests are very frustrating for young children, who are often able to provide very few of the missing words. Additionally, the characteristics of the passage used for the cloze test dramatically affect student performance. Background knowledge of the subject of a text makes more difference than anything else in how easy or difficult it is to comprehend the text, so the content of the text chosen for a cloze passage is of the utmost importance. Content becomes even more important for second language learners because cultural differences mean that shared background knowledge cannot be assumed. Cloze passages, however, are normally chosen based on grade-level readability formulas, and their content is rarely considered.

Sometimes **standardized achievement tests** are used to assess ability in written English and in content areas when evaluating a student for possible exit from a bilingual program. The problem with such tests is that, for many reasons, they underestimate the abilities of bilingual students. It is true that a child who can reach criterion level on a standardized achievement test will probably do well in a monolingual classroom where success is determined by performance on such tests. However, many children who are actually very proficient in school use of English may remain in bilingual programs longer than necessary and eventually be referred for special education programs because of these tests. (Remaining in a bilingual program longer than necessary would not be a negative if bilingual programs were not viewed as compensatory, if special education referrals were not so often the result of a failure to be mainstreamed, and if more provisions for integration with English-speaking children were built into the bilingual programs.)

Investigations

Test Assessment, p. 119.

Frank Smith (1986) provides a strong critique of the use of standardized testing with any students, not just those from different linguistic and cultural backgrounds. *Insult to Intelligence* is a powerful indictment of the damage done by testing systems that systematically sort children into "above average" and "below average." The system is set up so that 50 percent of children in American schools are likely to think they are "stupid" because their test scores show they are "below average." Teachers see low test scores from previous years and expect less of these children, who then acheive less due to the "self-fulfilling prophecy" of teacher expectations. These children may have many other abilities that are not reflected on standardized tests but never get a chance to prove to their teachers or to themselves that they can perform well in other ways.

Frameworks

Smith's book is also discussed in Authentic Purpose on p. 70 and Technology on p. 90.

There are other, less obvious results of overreliance on standardized testing. Teachers, whose performance is often assessed on the basis of their students' test scores, begin to "teach to the test." This results in more focus than ever on discrete skills, with a concomitant ignoring of holistic abilities and critical thinking skills. Both teachers and students begin to think that all questions have a single correct answer, which leads to a decrease in creativity and divergent thinking. Teachers, students and parents begin to believe that a person's abilities can be defined in terms of a number or a set of numbers, and the test becomes the thing it was meant to assess.

So far this discussion has centered on tests used to assess students for entry into and exit from bilingual or ESL programs. While students are in these programs their progress is measured through ongoing assessment of language proficiency and achievement in content areas. Procedures for such measurements can range from formal tests and quizzes to informal assessment by observation. Achievement tests that accompany commercial materials can be useful as diagnostic instruments if they do not focus exclusively on discrete point skills. Although teacher-made tests that meet the reliability and validity criteria of professional testmakers are difficult to construct, they can be very useful as diagnostic tools. In addition, short teacher-made quizzes provide practice in test taking and often serve as motivation for students to study. Observation of children doing academic tasks is the most valid way of finding out whether they are capable of the tasks. Observation is often not accepted as a valid form of assessment because of the claim that it is not objective. However, it can be made more objective by providing detailed descriptions of what students can actually do and by developing checklists that guide the observer in what to look for.

TeacherSource

More information about classroom language assessment can be found in *Dilemmas, Decisions and Directions* in the *TeacherSource* series.

Portfolios are increasingly being used in bilingual classrooms to document stu-

**Investigations**

Observe a
class in which
portfolios are
used. Interview
the teacher and
students to find
out how they feel
about this form
of assessment.

dents' progress over time. The most common area in which **portfolio assessment** is used is writing. Samples of students' writing, both drafts and final versions, are dated and kept in a file folder. The teacher consults the portfolio periodically to assess progress and inform instruction. Students should also have access to their portfolios so they can see the progress they are making. The portfolios provide a permanent record of students' abilities for demonstration to parents, administrators, and next year's teachers. Portfolios containing mathematics papers provide diagnostic information that is missing from test scores or checklists. In addition to products such as compositions and mathematics worksheets, portfolios can contain teachers' notes on student behaviors during the process of producing the products. A skill such as reading, which does not produce a product, is more difficult to document through portfolio assessment. A reading portfolio could contain products such as students' written responses to things they read, lists of books read with short comments, or art projects based on their readings. Similar products can be collected in science and social studies.

One of the great advantages of portfolio assessment for bilingual students is that it provides evidence of students' abilities as bilinguals without restricting them to one or the other of their languages. Documents are collected that show the use of both languages, either separately or together. For students who communicate best in a mixed code, their ability can be displayed in ways that no test would ever allow.

**Learning logs** kept by children can also be a source of ongoing informal assessment; they are valuable in showing students' growth in understanding over time. Writing entries in learning logs is also a learning tool that helps students articulate what they understand and what needs to be clarified. If they are used in a dialogue format they provide a way for teachers to clarify some of the things about which individual students express uncertainty.

**Investigations**

Observe a class
in which learning
logs are used.
Interview the
students to find
out what they
feel they learn
from keeping
the logs.

The process of assessment by observing, by collecting products and notes about process written by both students and teachers, and by reviewing journals kept by students about their own learning is very different from the process of assessment by achievement test. The former is a part of the learning process. Learning and evaluation are inseparable, so the evaluation includes the social interactions that many people believe are necessary for learning. It includes the enthusiasm that genuine learning generates in most students. The very process of assessment and evaluation leads to more learning. The latter (use of achievement tests) creates its own process, totally apart from any kind of learning. Students are forced to work individually, no matter what their preferred learning style might be. They are confronted with a complex procedure of reading items and choosing and marking the correct answer among several alternatives. This requires considerable practice just to learn the procedure, practice that students may or may not have had (and if they have had it, it is certainly a waste of time in terms of any kind of authentic learning). The items that form the test questions are chosen deliberately to be unfamiliar to students and then stripped of any context in order to force students to rely only on their comprehension skills to answer them. The use of background knowledge and context to understand all kinds of text, however, is one of the most beneficial comprehension skills students can develop.

Given the emphasis placed on achievement test results, the testing process often becomes more important than the learning process. It doesn't matter what you know, understand, appreciate, and value. All that matters is the extent to which you can second-guess the test writers by figuring out, in any way possible, which answer they think is correct. If you are from another culture, that second-guessing becomes nearly impossible, as cultural differences influence the interpretations you give to words, pictures, and situations.

I am one of those people who does well on standardized multiple-choice tests, and I have benefited academically from my facility in test-taking. Perhaps because of this, I am more aware than many people of the inequities created by overreliance on test scores. With my natural inclination to distrust standardized achievement test scores, I had a strong response to Edelsky and Harman's (1991) critique of testing—they make many of the same points as Smith (1986). What tests actually assess is similarity in the test taker's background knowledge to that of the people who wrote the test. Test scores are misleading because the process of norming scores means that what counts as a "passing" score can change over time, and the continued raising of scores becomes impossible. The tasks that students are asked to do on tests do not reflect what people actually do when they read with understanding. The use of test scores assumes that the abilities tested are permanent traits and that the way to increase people's abilities is to raise test scores. Testing not only takes time away from real learning but also forces the curriculum to reflect what the tests assess.

The effects of all of this are damaging even for students who do well on tests. For those who don't the effects are devastating because the supposedly objective nature of the tests makes it look as if there is something wrong with children who don't do well on them. As Cummins (1986, 1989) points out, the response of school systems is then to keep on testing the child until they find out what is "wrong." Eventually one of the tests will provide a label for the child, and teacher, child, and parents will come to believe that there really is something wrong with the child. What is actually wrong is an overreliance on one particular kind of test scores, to the exclusion of all other indicators of a child's abilities.

It will not be easy for teachers to resist the influence of standardized testing in this country. What is needed is for more and more teachers to begin to collect other kinds of evidence of children's abilities, including both language proficiency and academic achievement. As other teachers and administrators come to realize that alternative kinds of assessment are a better indication of students' abilities, perhaps our overreliance on standardized tests will diminish.

Case Study,
p. 119.

Classroom
Research, p. 119.

*Analyze Matilde's beliefs about testing as indicated by her classroom assessment practices and her views about achievement testing and criterion-referenced testing. How do these views compare with whole language approaches to testing?*

Reflection

## Suggested Readings:

*Key Works:* Edelsky and Harman (1991) and Smith (1986) gave me a theoretical basis for my deep distrust of standardized test results with bilingual children. Edelsky and Harman show how the very constructs on which literacy testing is based are faulty; Smith links testing to his critique of programmatic learning.

Valdés and Figueroa (1994) provide empirical research as well as theoretical arguments in making their case that the use of standardized testing with bilingual students constitutes bias.

Navarrete et al. (1990) and Pierce and O'Malley (1992) provide descriptions of alternative assessment for use with bilingual students. A more complete description of an alternative assessment program in use (although not with bilingual students) can be found in Woodward (1994).

## Culture is an integral part of both the curriculum and classroom organization

*Record ways that you remember experiencing cultural learning in school as a student or a teacher. Reflect on what you learned from these experiences, which ways of teaching culture you feel were most effective, and why they were effective.*

Journal

The incorporation of culture in Matilde's classroom is described on pp. 55-61.

The issue of how to make **bilingual education** bicultural as well has not been completely resolved. Many bilingual programs treat culture at the level of "folklore and festivals." Surface-level differences among the cultures represented in the classroom or the school are exploited in displays, art projects, and holiday celebrations. However, the presentation of a few highly visible features of colorful or exotic societies will not lead to an understanding of the dynamics of culture, and may even result in the formation of stereotypes. Such an approach tends to emphasize differences while providing little or no understanding of why they occur. The result is often the opposite of what is intended: Instead of a better understanding of other cultures, children may end up thinking that other people are very strange indeed.

Biculturalism must be an integral part of a bilingual education program, not something that is occasionally added on to the curriculum. Obviously, teaching a monolingual curriculum wholly or partially in another language does not result in a bicultural curriculum. Using stories about José instead of Joe, creating story problems about tacos instead of hamburgers, or adding and subtracting pesos and centavos instead of dollars and cents does nothing toward promoting biculturalism.

One popular approach to a bilingual/bicultural curriculum is the comparative study of the two cultures represented in the classroom (Almaraz, 1979). In this approach, whatever is studied about one culture is also studied about the other. If children engage in activities related to American holidays, they also engage in activities related to Hispanic (or other ethnic group) holidays. (If all the children are from the same country, the focus will be on that culture; if the children are from various countries, the focus will need to be broader.) If the students do a unit on the community, they compare an American community with an Hispanic community. This approach allows for an in-depth comparison of cultures, with the aim being that students will come to understand why there are differences and value both ways of doing things.

The problem with this comparative approach is that when it is taught within the domain of influence of only one of the cultures, it is very difficult for young children to be objective about the two cultures. This is especially true when one of the cultures has an overriding worldwide influence, as does the culture of the United States. It is almost impossible for a child's native culture to compete fairly in comparisons of this kind.

One way to avoid comparing United States culture with another culture is to study many different cultures. This is what Abbey (1973) suggests when she proposes that social studies for ESL students be taught as cultural anthropology. Arguing that the comparative study of cultures is more objective if a range of cultures is presented, she outlines a curriculum that focuses on nine different cultures representing a wide range of geographic environments, population sizes, racial groups, levels of subsistence, and language backgrounds. Four of the groups are bilingual, so students can see that they are not the only ones struggling with two languages, and two of the groups are bilingual in languages other than English. Each child's own culture(s) may or may not be among those presented. Each culture is represented by a child the same age as the learners, and the culture is explored from within, from that child's perspective. The aim is for students to understand the reasons that cultures differ.

Almost twenty years after I first read Abbey's article, I am still impressed with her ability to make complex concepts about culture understandable to young children. The basic structure of her curriculum is easy to adapt to whatever materials are available. The first time I adapted her curriculum, I happened to find a book that described how children live in eight different countries, and I used that book as a basis for learning about each culture. If I were teaching this curriculum now, I would begin by having the children suggest some of the cultures they wanted to learn about, and then have them help me collect materials about the cultures we chose together. This could be done using theme cycles as described in Involvement on pp. 87-88.

Biculturalism, of course, is not just the overt study of cultures. Culture is infused into everything that is done in a classroom. Even the absence of overt references to culture is an implicit cultural statement in itself. Teachers often ask how they can incorporate student culture into the classroom when their students come from many different cultures. The answer is that it is not the teacher who brings these many different cultures into the classroom, but the students. Students can bring in artifacts that relate to topics being discussed, although some may be reluctant to do this and should not be pushed if that is the case. A more fruitful approach is to express genuine interest in how and why things are done in certain ways in all students' cultures, encouraging them to share whenever it is appropriate in whatever way they can.

Case Study,
p. 120.

This kind of incorporation of the children's culture into all aspects of the curriculum is one of the four means of empowering minority students recommended by Jim Cummins (1986). Cummins's article strongly reinforced my belief that what teachers do really does make a difference. At the time I read the article, I was finding it increasingly difficult to ignore the preponderance of evidence showing the importance of societal and sociocultural factors in school success. I was becoming more and more discouraged about what teachers could realistically expect to accomplish when working with children who were deemed by society to be "at risk." The article affirmed my belief that there are things that teachers can do in spite of social pressures to ensure that "at-risk" students don't fail.

Two of the suggestions in Cummins's framework relate to the issue of culture within the classroom. They are the incorporation of student language and culture into the classroom, and the encouragement of community participation as an integral part of education.

It is often assumed that bilingual programs will automatically incorporate the students' languages and cultures into the classroom. This is not always the case. There are "bilingual" classrooms in which the only use of native languages is to discipline the children, and their cultures are virtually ignored. On the other hand, a program does not have to be "bilingual" in order to incorporate both language and culture. Perhaps the most important factor in the incorporation of language into the program is the teachers' and school's attitudes toward the use of the native language. Even classrooms that cannot use the children's native languages for instruction can establish an atmosphere in which all languages are welcomed and valued. Conversely, even in classrooms in which the native language is used almost exclusively, an attitude of celebration for learning a little bit of English, with no corresponding celebration for achievements in the native language, can result in students coming to believe that English is more important than the native language.

In thinking about the incorporation of culture into the classroom, it is important to remember that culture must be incorporated at the deep level of values and behaviors, not at the surface level of festivals and folklore, so that children can understand why their culture differs from that of the school. As with language, children's cultures are sometimes more readily accepted and made part of the classroom in a monolingual program than in some bilingual programs.

Cummins's second point is that community participation in programs for minority children must be encouraged. The importance of community participation in bilingual programs is usually more evident in theory than in practice. Although Parent Advisory Councils (PACs) are common, they may not be active, or they may be controlled by school personnel rather than by parents. Teachers can encourage parent participation by keeping parents informed of how their children are doing in school (telling them about the good as well as the bad), by encouraging participation in school-related activities that children do at home, and by maintaining an open-door policy for parents in their classrooms.

The two other elements of Cummins's framework have to do with pedagogy and assessment. Cummins advocates an interactive experiential approach to pedagogy, very similar to the meaning-based interactive pedagogy promoted in this book. He contrasts this with traditional **transmission teaching**. The transmission of "basic skills" not only contradicts what is known about how learning occurs, but also serves to maintain a sense of powerlessness in students. A more learner-centered approach to teaching is more likely to promote authentic learning, and also gives students greater control over their learning. An interactive/experiential approach can thus help empower students by showing them that they can control their own learning, in addition to contributing to greater learning and clearer understanding.

In assessment, Cummins contrasts advocacy-oriented and legitimization-oriented approaches. The latter locate the source of school failure in the students themselves. If students don't do well in school, it is assumed that there is something wrong with them. They are then tested until the "cause" of their "disability" is found. In an advocacy-oriented approach the focus is on looking at the context in which the child is learning, and in locating the causes of bilingual children's learning problems in other factors, such as subtractive approaches to language and culture, exclusionary policies toward the child's community, and transmission approaches to pedagogy.

In all of these areas, individual teachers who are willing to confront the power structure of the schools can make a difference. In the book that is an

Assessment, pp. 101-106, deals with these issues in more depth.

extension of his earlier article, Cummins (1989) shows how various projects that employ **critical literacy, cooperative learning,** and **process writing** are having positive effects on the education of bilingual students.

One of these projects is the implementation of a bilingual science program called *Descubrimiento/Finding Out* in Passaic, New Jersey. The program itself facilitates experimentation and language development through small-group activities based on materials in both Spanish and English. Children read, discuss, evaluate, and write in the language of their choice. In this particular case, when parents were shown the program to demonstrate to them what their children were doing in school, many of them expressed the desire to complete the program themselves. The parents were then trained to use the program, and it became a vehicle for them to learn English. Several of the parents who participated in the program ended up working as classroom assistants (*Public Education Institute Quarterly,* 1987, cited in Cummins, 1989).

The second project described by Cummins involved parents sharing in their children's literacy development. This was the Pájaro Valley Family Literacy Project, developed by Alma Flor Ada (1988). This project was designed to encourage parental participation. Meetings were held in the library, which was considered more nonthreatening than the school; parents were asked to participate through written invitation; a parallel program for children was offered at the same time. At the first meeting, the importance of native language development and pride in their own culture was discussed. The parents chose children's books to read to their children at home, and then met in small groups to read and discuss the books. In subsequent meetings they recounted their experiences discussing these books with their children, read stories their children had written, and chose and discussed new books. Their readings of the books they had chosen and of their children's stories was videotaped. The parents began to borrow the videos to watch at home and to show their friends and families, which helped the children learn to read the books they saw their parents reading on the tapes, and also increased their motivation to write more (Brown, 1993).

The third program described by Cummins is the use of telecommunications to promote native language literacy and cultural pride. He describes the *Orillas* computer network (*De Orilla a Orilla*—From Shore to Shore) that links classes of bilingual students in the United States with "**sister classes**" of Spanish speakers in Hispanic countries (Sayers, 1993; Sayers and Brown, 1987). He also talks about programs developed by Estéban Díaz and Luis Moll in San Diego and Pedro Pedraza in New York in which children and their parents can work on computers together after school. In New York the community controls the project completely, and the computers are being used to produce income and publications for the community. The *Orillas* network has also been used for a project involving parents in California (Brown, 1993). Parent and child partners were enrolled in an after-school computer course. The group included a wide range of ages, languages, English proficiency, and literacy skills. Instruction was difficult at first, with a notable lack of patience among the English-speaking parents during the time when instruction was being translated. However, attitudes changed when the electronic communication began. The status of the Spanish speakers in the group rose as they were needed to translate messages received in

More information about both the *Orillas* project and the use of telecommunications in bilingual classrooms is found in Technology on pp. 90-93.

Spanish, and the English speakers became more patient with translation as they themselves experienced the need for it. The group became more cohesive as they worked together on a book to be sent to their "sister class" in Denver.

In all of these successful projects, there is an affirmation of the culture of the participants. Parents and children work together on projects that are based on the parents' language and culture, thus portraying that culture as something to take pride in and maintain, rather than something to be left behind in the process of Americanization. Teachers must bring their students' cultures into the class in ways that are connected to the literacy development and knowledge development that go on there. Culture can then become an integral part of the classroom, not something to be studied only, not something to be celebrated on holidays only, but something to live and be proud of.

Classroom Research, pp. 120.

*Think about the ways in which Matilde brings culture into her classroom, both explicitly and implicitly. Compare these with what you do, or might do, in your own classroom.*

Reflection

## Suggested Readings:

*Key Works:* Abbey's (1973) short outline of a social studies curriculum and Cummins's (1986, 1989) powerful framework for *Empowering Minority Students*, although quite different from each other, have both influenced my thoughts about the place of culture in bilingual education. Abbey was my first exposure to the idea of teaching culture from within; Cummins gave me hope that by incorporating culture into the classroom, bilingual teachers could empower their students.

Ovando and Collier (1985) give a comprehensive overview of the many facets of culture that are involved in bilingual education. Jordan (1995) shows how cultural factors affect student achievement and describes programs designed to take those factors into consideration.

# ENDING:
# ABOUT CHANGE

Bilingual children are among those who have been categorized by society as "at risk" for success in school. Children are presumed to be "at risk" if they speak a language other than English, if their skin is a color other than white, if their socioeconomic background is other than middle or upper class, or if their preschool experiences are other than what the school assumes all children have had.

I do not believe that children are "at risk" because of whatever characteristics they do or do not possess. Rather, if certain children are "at risk," it is because schools have failed to provide the kinds of programs that will ensure their success. Whether this is due to intentional gatekeeping on the part of society or to misguided efforts by educators does not really matter. What matters is that schools change in order to truly provide equal educational opportunity for all.

Change in schools can occur through top-down or bottom-up reform. Top-down reform often has very little real effect on schools. The reforms suggested may not correspond to the real problems of the schools. Teachers may be too suspicious of reforms imposed from above to implement them effectively. Those in power may have a vested interest in actually maintaining the status quo while giving the appearance of trying to implement change. Top-down educational reform often results in very little real change at the classroom level.

On the other hand, bottom-up reform has the potential to transform schools. Ultimately, teachers are the only ones who can implement reforms in ways that ensure success. They have the greatest interest in making schools work. Bottom-up change can take a long time, occurring in small increments and affecting only one classroom at a time as it spreads from teacher to teacher. In the long run, however, it can fundamentally change the ways in which schools deal with all children.

This book has concentrated on bottom-up reform, suggesting ways in which classroom teachers can structure their classrooms in order to reduce the risk of failure for bilingual students (or others who are also considered "at risk"). I am not suggesting that individual teachers can overcome all of the societal problems that contribute to school success or failure. I am, however, suggesting that there are a great many things teachers can do to work toward greater success for all their students.

There is evidence that the kinds of authentic student-centered approaches advocated in this book lead to increased achievement for bilingual students. Collier found that "students achieve significantly better in programs that teach...through cognitively complex content, taught through problem-solving, discovery learning in highly interactive calssroom activities" (1995a, p. 9).

Teachers must be cautioned, however, not to try to change too much in their classrooms at one time. Substantial changes cannot occur in a short period because change requires time for planning, adjustments, and reflection. It is best to begin on a small scale, moving gradually toward more authenticity of tasks and more student involvement. Many of the teachers I have worked with have begun to make changes by instituting **dialogue journals**, which require minimal adjustment to existing classroom routines but make a big difference in terms of authentic use of language and personalization of tasks.

Another danger that teachers implementing change can run into is to create an ideal in their minds that they can never live up to. Because they perceive that they cannot be the teacher they envision, they give up any idea at all of change. One of the lessons I learned by observing in Matilde's classroom is that every teacher must implement change in ways that are consistent with his or her own understanding. Matilde's ways of implementing a **whole language** approach were different from how I would have done it, or how any other teacher would have done it. But they were consistent with Matilde's understandings of what she needed to be doing with her students at that time. No approach, whether it's whole language, **cooperative learning,** or another, is a question of "all or nothing," and no two teachers will implement these approaches in exactly the same way. Nobody can say that the way a particular teacher does something is "wrong."

If we believe in our students and ourselves we can quietly revolutionize the ways in which classroom teachers approach students. No students need to be considered "at risk," and no students need to fail because the school did not meet their needs. We can open the gates of opportunity for those students who used to find them closed because their backgrounds did not match the school's expectations.

Teachers can explore their own and other teachers' decision-making processes with the *Teachers Understanding Teaching* CD-ROM in the *TeacherSource* series.

Pages 61-62 discuss some of the contradictions in Matilde's approach to teaching.

# INVESTIGATIONS

*Bilingual children learn in the same ways as other children*

**Case Study:** Prepare a case study dealing with the likelihood of success in school of one of the three children described on pages 14-20. You might address the following issues, among others:

- whether this child could be considered a "successful" second grader
- what factors go into determining what a "successful" student is
- what predictions might be made about this child's future
- what kind of school program might improve this child's chances for success

p. 20.

**Classroom Research:** Write brief notes on how you think a particular student spends his or her time during a typical day in your classroom or in a classroom you are observing. Then record how this student actually spends his or her time (videotape the student if possible; if not, observe and take detailed notes, or have somebody else observe and take notes). Compare your original notes with the reality of what the student does. If you think the reality needs to be changed, plan ways to do that. If the child is in your own classroom, keep notes about what occurs as you implement changes.

p. 66.

*Children learn when they are doing something that has an authentic purpose*

**Discourse Analysis:** Analyze the reading comprehension review session on pages 26-28 and the continuation of that session in the Appendix. What do you think Matilde's intention with each of her questions and statements is? What function does each actually serve? What underlying beliefs about reading comprehension are reflected in these interactions?

p. 28.

**Case Study:** Prepare a case study of a teacher whose students write in journals every day but who wants to make the journal writing more authentic. Issues you could address include:

- who the audience for the journals is
- whether and how journals should be used for the correction of mechanics
- how the content of the journals is determined

p. 68.

p. 71.

**Classroom Research:** Think about what kinds of reading and writing activities students in an "ideal" classroom should do. Then keep notes about the kinds of activities they actually do in your classroom or in a classroom you are observing. Review your notes and make a list of things you would like to change. If it is your own classroom, implement some of the changes and observe what happens as you do.

## Children learn by doing

p. 37.

**Case Study:** Choose one of the three subject areas discussed and develop a case study of a teacher who wants to move into more "learning by doing" in that subject. Some of the issues you might want to address include:

- what "learning by doing" really means for that subject
- how teachers with minimal training in the subject can move away from teaching from textbooks
- availability of resource materials
- dealing with student reactions to major changes in procedures

p. 78.

**Activities Continuum:** Make a list of mathematics, science, and social studies activities you have observed, used, or read about (including those you read about in Matilde's clasroom and the suggestions for learning by doing given in the Frameworks strand—you may want to read the original sources of those suggestions for more detail about what actually happened in the classrooms described). For each subject, create a continuum of activities you have observed or read about, from the most student-activity oriented to the most teacher-transmission oriented. Where do most of the activities on your list fall on the continuum? Why do you think this is so?

p. 78.

**Classroom Research:** Choose one of the three content areas—mathematics, science, or social studies—and decide on the most appropriate activities for students in that subject. Then observe the activities that students actually do during their content lessons in your classroom or in a classroom you are observing. Are there activities you should change? Make a list of them and, if it is your own classroom, implement some of the changes, observing what happens as you do.

## Children learn when their teachers believe in them, in themselves, and in what they are doing

p. 84.

**Case Study:** Prepare case studies of teachers who are concerned that they have low expectations for some students; they want to find out whether they do indeed have low expectations, and if so, to find ways to change them. You might address the following issues, among others:

- how teachers know whether they have low expectations for particular students
- the difference between low expectations and a realistic assessment of a low-functioning student's ability
- how teachers convey high or low expectations to students
- specific things teachers might do if they find that they do indeed have low expectations for some students

**Classroom Research:** Think about your own theories of learning. Then examine your teaching practices to see whether they coincide with your theories of learning. This could be done through a two-part journal. On the left side of each page, record short descriptions of various techniques and activities that you implement in the classroom. Periodically review what you have written, and on the right side of each page, note the theory of learning that is reflected in your practices. Does this "reflected" theory agree with what you profess to believe? If not, plan ways in which you could bring your theory and your practices more in line with each other. As you implement changes, observe and record what happens.

p. 85.

If you are observing in somebody else's classroom, interview the teacher about theories of learning and how they are implemented in his or her classroom. Then compare the teacher's statements with what you have observed. To what extent do the teacher's practices agree with his or her beliefs? If they don't, give possible reasons for the discrepancy. Do the teacher's practices agree with your beliefs? Make a list of what you would change if it were your classroom.

### *Children learn when they are involved in determining what and how they will learn*

**Case Study:** Prepare a case study of a beginning bilingual teacher who learned how to plan through thematic units or theme cycles during preservice training but feels so overwhelmed during the first year of teaching that he or she doesn't know where to begin. You might address issues such as:

p. 88.

- the advantages and disadvantages of teaching from thematic units or theme cycles versus teaching from textbooks
- what can realistically be expected of a teacher in terms of how much time he or she spends planning instruction
- ways in which the planning for thematic units or theme cycles could be simplified

**Classroom Research:** Reflect on what you believe to be the most appropriate ways to plan your teaching. Then record your own planning processes. What factors influence the ways in which you plan? What, if anything, would you like to change about the ways in which you plan? What steps could you take to implement any changes you might want to make? As you implement changes, record anything that happens in the classroom that might be related to the changes you made in your planning processes.

p. 88.

If you are observing in somebody else's classroom, interview the teacher about the planning process. To what extent and how does he or she involve students in planning, either directly or indirectly? What are the benefits and/or the drawbacks of involving students in planning? Observe a class and note any effects of involving students in planning. Make a list of principles about planning to keep in mind for your own classroom.

### *Children learn when they have control over the technology used to help them learn*

**Telecommunications Project:** Find out how you could get access to a telecommunications network. Talk with your school media specialist or with people in the com-

p. 92.

puter center of your college or university. Access a bulletin board, list, discussion group, or World Wide Web page that matches classes for telecommunications projects, and choose a project that you would like to pursue.

p. 92.

**Case Study:** Develop a case study of a teacher with limited computer experience who has just been given four computers for his or her classroom. You could address issues such as:

- the optimal uses of this number of computers in one classroom
- the types of software would that be most useful
- how a teacher with limited experience with computers can learn to use them effectively

p. 93.

**Classroom Research:** Develop a plan for what you would consider to be the optimum use of the computers that are available to you. Then think about how those computers are actually used. Does your use of computers fit with your beliefs about how children learn? Are there ways in which you can bring your actual computer use more in line with your optimum plan? Plan changes you could make and keep notes of what happens as you implement the changes. If you do not have access to computers, plan ways in which you will use them when they become available.

If you are observing in somebody else's classroom, take notes on how computers are used in that classroom. Do you believe this is the most effective way they could be used in this situation? List ways in which you would use them differently if this were your classroom. If you feel that the teacher you are observing would be open to your ideas, discuss them with him or her. If any changes are made, observe what happens.

*The amount of use of each language, and the ways in which each is used, should be consciously determined*

p. 48.

**Discourse Analysis:** Analyze Matilde's use of Spanish and English as shown throughout the Teachers' Voices strand with respect to the following questions and any others you may have:

- What patterns, if any, do you see in the choices Matilde makes about which language to use?
- What possible reasons might you suggest for the codeswitches you find?
- How does Matilde's actual language use relate to her expressed views on language use as described on page 46?

p. 97.

**Case Study:** Prepare a case study of a bilingual teacher who has been using concurrent translation or random switching in his or her classroom and is not satisfied with that approach. Issues you might address include:

- why concurrent translation and random switching are not effective
- the alternatives
- factors that an individual teacher needs to take into account when making decisions about language use
- how easily and effectively the decisions the teacher makes can be implemented

**Classroom Research:** Write down what you consider to be the most appropriate ways to use two languages in a bilingual classroom. Then make notes about how you think you actually use them, or how a teacher you are observing uses them. Finally, record actual language use, either through audio or videotaping or through observing and detailed note taking. Compare your ideal with what you thought the reality was and with what the reality is. If there are discrepancies, why do you think they occur? If this is your own classroom, plan and implement changes you could make to bring the reality closer to the ideal and observe what happens when you implement the changes.

p. 99.

*Children must be assessed in ways that reflect both
natural language use and the ways in which they learn*

**Test Assessment:** Examine a language dominance or language proficiency test or a standardized achievement test that might be used with bilingual students. If possible, give the test, or at least portions of it, to a bilingual student. Compare what the test purports to measure with what it actually measures. Also compare what the results of the test show about the student's ability with what you know about that ability. Discuss your findings with a teacher who has used the test and see if your assessment agrees with his or hers.

p. 103.

**Case Study:** Prepare a case study of a student who performs well in school but does not do well on standardized tests. You might discuss issues such as the following:

- how the student can do well in school if he or she does not do well on standardized tests
- what the likely effects of this situation are
- what steps a teacher could take to try to ensure that the student's poor performance on standardized tests does not negatively affect his or her school career

p. 105.

**Classroom Research:** Think about how you would ideally want to assess your students' language proficiency and academic achievement. Then list all the procedures, both formal and informal, that are used to assess them in your classroom or in the classroom you are observing. Are there procedures on your list that you think are not useful? Are there procedures that should be on your list that aren't? If this is your classroom, make a list of the steps you can take to bring your assessment procedures more in line with what you believe they should be. Implement some of those steps and observe what happens. If you are observing in somebody else's classroom, discuss with the teacher why assessment occurs as it does.

p. 105.

*Culture is an integral part of both
the curriculum and classroom organization*

**Incorporating Culture:** Despite the atmosphere of cultural congruence in Matilde's class, there is very little overt reference to culture. Reread "The Teacher," pp. 13-62, and make notes of instances in which culture could have been incorporated into the curriculum but wasn't. Then generalize your notes into a list of suggestions for incorporating culture into a bilingual classroom.

p. 61.

p. 108.

**Case Study:** Develop a case study of a bilingual teacher who is fluent in the language of his or her students but has limited direct experience with their culture. You might address such issues as the following:

- the extent to which it is necessary for teachers to have experienced the culture of their students
- how a lack of cultural congruence might affect classroom interactions
- ways in which the teacher could increase his or her experience with the students' culture if necessary

p. 111.

**Classroom Research:** Make notes of the ways in which you would want culture to be reflected in your classroom. Then list all the manifestations of culture—explicit and implicit—that you can think of in your classroom or in the classroom you are observing. Compare your "ideal" notes with the "reality" list, and decide what you would want to change. If this is your classroom, make plans for ways to implement changes and observe what happens when you do.

# *Appendix*

Transcript of the question/answer session that followed the reading and discussion of the homework reading comprehension sheet on snakes (the text of the reading passage and accompanying questions is found on pp. 26-29):

*Teacher: OK, ¿entendieron lo que leímos ahora? ¿De qué leímos ahora?*

*Child: Una serpiente.*

*T: Estamos hablando de una serpiente. ¿Qué es una cosa que leímos sobre la serpiente?*

*C: (unintelligible)*

*T: ¿Qué más hablaron de ese animal? ¿Qué más? ¿Hablaron del tamaño de la serpiente?*

*C: No.*

*T: Hablaron, ¿no? Sí. ¿Cómo es el cuerpo de la serpiente?*

*C: Flaco.*

*T: Largo y flaco. OK. ¿Hablaron del color?*

*C: No.*

*T: No sabemos qué es el color de esa serpiente. Pero sí sabemos que hace un hoyo. ¿Qué más? ¿Se puede doblar?*

*C: Sí.*

*T: ¿Sin problemas?*

*C: Sí.*

*T: ¿Qué más? ¿Alguien ha visto a esa serpiente salir del hoyo para atrás?*

*C: No.*

*T: OK, vamos a las preguntas. Tienen que leer las instrucciones. Dice que marquen el círculo al*

Teacher: OK, did you understand what we read now? What did we read about now?

Child: A snake.

T: We are talking about a snake. What's one thing that we read about the snake?

C: (unintelligible)

T: What else did they say about that animal? What else? Did they talk about the size of the snake?

C: No.

T: They talked about it, didn't they? Yes. What's the body of the snake like?

C: Thin.

T: Long and thin. OK. Did they talk about the color?

C: No.

T: We don't know what color that snake is. But we do know that it makes a hole. What else? Can it bend?

C: Yes.

T: Without any problem?

C: Yes.

T: What else? Has anybody seen that snake coming out of the hole backwards?

C: No.

T: OK, let's go to the questions. You have to read the instructions. It says you should mark the circle

lado de la respuesta correcta.
*Aquí tienen cuatro respuestas; las
cuatro no son correctas: yendo
para atrás, de cabeza, como
entró, pequeño. Sabiendo lo que
han leído sobre ese animal, ¿cuál
es la respuesta correcta?*

C: *Yendo para atrás.*

T: *¿Quién puede encontrar dónde
dice la respuesta?*

C: *En el párrafo tres.*

T: *Léeme la respuesta solamente.*

C: (reading) *Nadie ha visto a una
serpiente salir de un hoyo yendo
para atrás.*

T: *Allí está la respuesta, ella la
encontró en el párrafo tres. ¿Hay
pregunta? Vamos a la segunda.
(reading) El cuento no habla del
cuerpo de la serpiente, del color
de la serpiente, de cómo da la
vuelta la serpiente, de los hoyos
en que se mete la serpiente.*

C: *Del color de la serpiente.*

T: *El cuento no habla del color de la
serpiente. ¿En qué párrafo está
esa información? No lo dice,
¿verdad? OK, número tres. Yo
quiero que Uds. estén corrigiendo
ahora, por favor. OK, vamos al
tres. (reading) Escribe Sí después
de cada oración que es verdad.
Escribe No después de cada
oración que no es verdad. ¿Qué
tenemos que hacer? Dime.*

C: *Hay que poner Sí si la oración es
verdad, y poner No si no es verdad.*

T: *¿Todos comprendieron eso?*

C: *Sí.*

T: (reading) *Una serpiente nunca se
mete en un hoyo pequeño.*

C: *No.*

T: *No, la respuesta es no. ¿Dónde*

next to the correct answer. You
have four answers here; the four
are not correct: backwards, head
first, like it went in, that is small.
Knowing what you have read
about that animal, which is the
correct answer?

C: Backwards.

T: Who can find where it says the
answer?

C: In paragraph three.

T: Read me only the answer.

C: (reading) Nobody has seen a snake
come out of a hole backwards.

T: There is the answer, she found it
in paragraph three. Any questions? Let's go to the second.
(reading) The story doesn't talk
about the body of the snake, the
color of the snake, how the snake
turns around, the holes that the
snake goes into.

C: The color of the snake.

T: The story doesn't talk about the
color of the snake. In which paragraph is that information? It
doesn't say it, right? OK, number
three. I want you to be correcting
now, please. OK, let's go to three.
(reading) Write yes after each sentence that is true. Write no after
each sentence that is not true.
What do we have to do? Tell me.

C: You have to put yes if the sentence
is true, and put no if it's not true.

T: Did everybody understand that?

C: Yes.

T: (reading) A snake never goes into
a small hole.

C: No.

T: No, the answer is no. Where is the

está la oración donde encuentran esa información? ¿Encontraron? Porque es fácil. Dime, Mariana.

C: *En el párrafo dos.*

T: *¿En el párrafo dos? ¿Dónde? Jorge. Vamos a ver.*

C: *En el párrafo uno.*

T: *En el párrafo uno. Léelo, por favor.*

C: (reading) *A veces vemos a una serpiente meterse en un hoyo muy chiquito.*

T: *¿Estamos de acuerdo? OK. All right, vamos a la segunda. (reading) Una serpiente puede dar la vuelta en un cuartito debajo de la tierra. ¿Sí o no?*

C: *Sí.*

T: *¿Estamos de acuerdo? Entonces vamos a ver dónde encontramos esa información.*

C: *En el párrafo uno.*

T: *Vamos a buscar todavía. Yo creo que hay otro párrafo que nos ayuda mejor a saber eso.*

C: *Párrafo dos.*

T: *En el párrafo dos. OK, ¿puedes leer dónde lo dice?*

C: (reading) *La serpiente va al cuartito y da la vuelta.*

T: *OK. ¿Estamos de acuerdo? (reading) Una serpiente sale de un hoyo de cabeza. ¿Sí o no?*

C: *Sí.*

T: *Sí, porque lo dice allí. ¿En cuál párrafo?*

C: *Dos.*

T: *¿En el párrafo dos? ¿En el párrafo dos? Yo creo que hay otro párrafo que nos da la información mejor. Dijimos que una serpiente sale de cabeza, pero ¿cómo sabemos? ¿Dónde encontramos la información? ¿Cómo entra?*

sentence where you find that information? Did you find it? Because it's easy. Tell me, Mariana.

C: In paragraph two.

T: In paragraph two? Where? Jorge. Let's see.

C: In paragraph one.

T: In paragraph one. Read it, please.

C: (*reading*) Sometimes we see a snake go into a very small hole.

T: Do we agree? OK. All right, let's go to the second one. (reading) A snake can turn around in a little room under the ground. Yes or no?

C: Yes.

T: Do we agree? Then let's see where we find that information.

C: In paragraph one.

T: Let's look some more. I think there's another paragraph that better helps us to know that.

C: Paragraph two.

T: In paragraph two. OK, can you read where it says it?

C: (*reading*) The snake goes to the little room and turns around.

T: OK. Do we agree? (*reading*) A snake comes out of a hole head first. Yes or no?

C: Yes.

T: Yes, because it says so there. In which paragraph?

C: Two.

T: In paragraph two? In paragraph two? I think there's another paragraph that gives us the information better. We said that a snake comes out head first, but how do we know? Where do we find the information? How does it go in?

C: *De cabeza.*

T: *Entra de cabeza. ¿Cómo sale? Vamos a mirar en el párrafo tres.*

C: *(reading) Nadie ha visto una serpiente salir de un hoyo yendo para atrás. Sale como entró, de cabeza.*

T: *Sale como entró, de cabeza. ¿Estamos de acuerdo? OK. Vamos a la cuatro. Tacha... Tacha. Uds. entienden la palabra 'tacha', ¿verdad? (reading) Tacha la palabra que no va con las otras. OK. Diara.*

C: *Dar.*

T: *¿Dar? ¿Dar? Antes de que Uds. empiecen a tachar, tienen que mirar las cuatro palabras. Esas son palabras que salen en el cuento.*

C: *Hoyo.*

T: *¿Hoyo? ¿Hoyo? ¿Hoyo no sale en el cuento?*

C: *Ver.*

T: *Ver. Sí, ver. Ver no sale en el cuento. Número cinco. (reading) Haz un círculo alrededor del número del párrafo que habla del cuerpo de la serpiente. ¿Quién lo tiene? ¿Ignacio?*

C: *Párrafo tres.*

T: *Número tres, que habla del cuerpo de la serpiente. OK, número tres, porque dice que su cuerpo es flaco.*

C: *Párrafo dos.*

T: *Número dos en sí no habla del cuerpo. No da descripciones. So it should be, en cinco, número tres. OK, número seis. (reading) Escribe la palabra del párrafo uno que significa "entrar."*

C: Head first.

T: It goes in head first. How does it come out? Let's look in paragraph three.

C: *(reading)* Nobody has seen a snake come out of a hole backwards. It comes out as it went in, head first.

T: It comes out as it went in, head first. Do we agree? OK. Let's go to four. Cross out... Cross out. You understand the word 'cross out', right? *(reading)* Cross out the word that does not go with the others. OK. Diara.

C: Give.

T: Give? Give? Before you begin to cross off, you have to look at all four words. Those are words that appear in the story.

C: Hole.

T: Hole? Hole? Hole doesn't appear in the story?

C: See.

T: See. Yes, see. See doesn't appear in the story. Number five. *(reading)* Make a circle around the number of the paragraph that talks about the body of the snake. Who has it? Ignacio?

C: Paragraph three.

T: Number three, that talks about the body of the snake. OK, number three, because it says that its body is thin.

C: Paragraph two.

T: Number two in itself doesn't talk about the body. It doesn't give descriptions. So it should be, in five, number three. OK, number six. *(reading)* Write the word from paragraph one that means "to enter."

C: *Meterse.*

T: *¿Cuántos hicieron esa parte correcto? ¿Tú no lo hiciste bien? ¿Qué pusiste?*

C: *Na'.*

T: *¿Nada?* You skipped it? It's better not to skip things because it's right there in the story. *Número siete. (reading) Gordo es lo contrario de...*

C: *Flaco.*

T: *Flaco, sí. Yo no encuentro que eso sea difícil. Es leer y comprender. Al principio lo que tienen que hacer es leer en silencio, y vuelven a leer en voz alta, pensando en lo que están leyendo.*

C: To go in.

T: How many did that part correctly? You didn't do it right? What did you put?

C: Nuttin'.

T: Nothing? You skipped it? It's better not to skip things because it's right there in the story. Number seven. (*reading*) Fat is the opposite of...

C: Thin.

T: Thin, yes. I don't find that difficult. It's reading and understanding. First what you have to do is read silently, and then go back and read out loud, thinking about what you're reading.

# Glossary

**Action research:** A term used to describe research undertaken by teachers in their own classrooms to study what happens in their teaching and their students' learning so they can make changes that will make them more effective teachers.

**Additive bilingualism:** A situation in which a bilingual's first language continues to develop while he or she is learning a second language. This continuing development of the first language provides a better basis for second language development than does *subtractive bilingualism*, in which the first language does not continue to develop after exposure to a second language.

**Basal reader:** A series of graded books used to teach reading, usually accompanied by workbooks and other supplementary materials. Traditional basal readers were carefully controlled for reading level and vocabulary load, and the quality of the stories was often mediocre. More recently, the content of basal readers has come to include quality children's literature.

**Basic skills:** A term used for instruction in the component sub-skills that contribute to ability in mathematics, reading, and writing. Competence in these areas is broken down into its smallest parts, which are taught in a decontexualized manner.

**Big book:** An enlarged book, usually with a limited amount of text on each page and a repetitive pattern. The book is read many times so the children become familiar with the text. By following along with the enlarged text, they begin to make associations between the oral words in the story they have learned and the printed words on the page.

**Bilingual education:** An educational program in which two languages are used as mediums of instruction. Around the world, many bilingual education programs are enrichment programs so middle- and upper-class children can enjoy the benefits of bilingualism. In the United States, most bilingual education programs are transitional in nature, meant to move linguistic minority children into all-English instruction as quickly as possible.

**Cloze test:** A test in which words are randomly deleted from a reading passage (every seventh or ninth word is most common); the person taking the test is asked to fill in the deletions. Cloze tests have been used as tests of basic language proficiency and reading level.

**Codeswitching:** A feature of bilingual speech in which the speaker changes from one language to the other. Codeswitching can occur between or within clauses or sentences and may comprise a single word, a phrase, a sentence, several sentences, or longer stretches of discourse.

**Constructivism:** A theory of learning that states that knowledge is constructed by the learner through social interaction, rather than being transmitted from an outside source to the learner.

**Cooperative learning:** A structure for classroom learning that makes use of group learning tasks that are designed so learners are mutually interdependent. The task cannot be accomplished unless everyone in the group participates.

**Criterion-referenced test:** A type of standardized (or nonstandardized) test that compares the test-taker's scores to specific criteria from the curriculum, rather than comparing them to the scores of others who have taken the same test (which is done with *norm-referenced tests*).

**Critical literacy:** A philosophy that sees literacy as more than the ability to read and write. Literacy is seen as the ability to understand the world and enables the literate person to take action to improve his or her position in the world.

**Critical pedagogy:** A kind of teaching based on critical literacy. Teaching and learning should result in action that will improve the learner's position in the world.

**Dialogue journal:** A two-way journal in which a teacher and student or two students conduct a conversation on paper. Each responds to what the other has written before continuing his or her own journal entry.

**Ethnographer:** A researcher who uses anthropological investigation techniques.

**Internet:** A vast network of interconnected computers and smaller computer networks that allows almost instantaneous communication between two computers anywhere in the world.

**Key words:** A technique for learning to read words, developed by Sylvia Ashton-Warner, in which each child chooses one very important word each day. The teacher writes the word on a card, and if the word is important enough, the child will learn to read it instantaneously.

**Language dominance:** The notion that one of a bilingual's two languages is stronger than the other. Many bilingual programs give incoming students tests that supposedly assess their language dominance; placement in a bilingual or monolingual program is determined by the results of such a dominance test.

**Language experience approach:** A way of teaching beginning reading in which a child dictates sentences about an experience he or she has had, the teacher or another person records the dictated sentences, and the child then reads them back. Language experience stories are also done with groups of children dictating sentences about a shared experience.

**Learning logs:** Journals in which the focus of the entry is on what the student has learned about a particular subject. They may also be done in dialogue journal format.

**Portfolio assessment:** A method of assessing performance by collecting samples of students' work.

**Predictable book:** A book in which a repeated pattern, a very familiar story, rhymes, or illustrations make it easy to guess which words come next. Predictable books are often used in enlarged form as big books for teaching beginning reading.

**Pre-primer:** The first book of a basal reading series. Traditional pre-primers contained very few words, either memorized sight words or words with regular phonetic patterns, which were repeated many times in each story. The simplification and vocabulary control made the stories uninteresting and difficult to make sense of.

**Process writing:** An approach to writing that uses pre-writing activities, writing and revision of multiple drafts, and often peer editing, to teach students that good writing is not the result of a single draft.

**Shared reading:** The technique of using a book with enlarged print so a group of children can all see the print. The teacher or other adult reads the story out loud several times, running a finger or a pointer under the corresponding words. The children listen and join in with the reading when they can.

**Sister classes:** A term used to describe two classes that are paired up for joint projects. Sister classes often use computers and telecommunications for faster sharing, but this isn't essential.

**Sound-symbol correspondence:** The connection between the written letter on the page and the sound that it represents when spoken.

**Standardized achievement test:** A standardized test that is based on grade-level norms for reading and content areas. Most school systems give all children standardized achievement tests approximately every three years; some give them every year.

**Standardized test:** A test that has been subjected to extensive reliability and validity studies. Most standardized tests are norm-referenced, which means that the tests are given to many people to establish norms against which test takers' scores can be compared.

**Thematic unit:** A teaching unit in which several different subject areas are integrated around a common theme.

**Theme cycle:** A way of teaching in which unanswered questions from one unit form the basis for the development of the next unit.

**Transmission teaching:** A view of teaching that assumes that knowledge exists outside the learner and that knowledge can be conveyed to the learner through a teacher or a textbook.

**Whole language:** An approach to language teaching that begins with larger units of language, looking at discrete sentences, words, or sounds only in the context of a larger text. It also integrates the four language skills and integrates language with other subject areas.

# References

Abbey, K. L. 1973. Social studies as social anthropology: A model for ESL curricula. *TESOL Quarterly* 7: 249-258.

Ada, A. F. 1988. The Pajaro Valley experience: Working with Spanish-speaking parents to develop children's reading and writing skills in the home through the use of children's literature. In *Minority education: From shame to struggle,* edited by T. Skutnabb-Kangas and J. Cummins. Clevedon, England: Multilingual Matters.

Almaraz, F. D., Jr. 1979. Social studies: A curricular cornerstone in bilingual education. In *Bilingual multicultural education and the professional: From theory to practice,* edited by H. T. Trueba and C. Barnett-Mizrahi. Rowley, MA: Newbury House Publishers.

Anthony, E. M. 1963. Approach, method, and technique. *English Language Teaching* 17: 63-67.

Ashton-Warner, S. 1963. *Teacher.* New York: Simon & Schuster.

Bilingual Education Office. 1990. *Bilingual education handbook: Designing instruction for LEP students.* Sacramento, CA: California Department of Education.

Brisk, M. 1985. Using the computer to develop literacy. *Equity and Choice* 1(3): 25-32.

Brown, C. 1978. *Literacy in 30 hours: Paulo Freire's process in northeast Brazil.* Berkeley, CA: Center for Open Learning and Teaching, Inc.

Brown, K. 1993. Balancing the tools of technology with our own humanity: The use of technology in building partnerships and communities. In *The power of two languages: Literacy and biliteracy for Spanish-speaking students,* edited by J. V. Tinajero and A. F. Ada. New York: Macmillan/McGraw-Hill School Publishing.

Carrasco, R. L. 1981. Expanded awareness of student performance: A case study in applied ethnographic monitoring in a bilingual classroom. In *Culture and the bilingual classroom: Studies in classroom ethnography,* edited by H. T. Trueba, G. P. Guthrie, and K. H.-P. Au. Rowley, MA: Newbury House Publishers.

Castro, E., Y. de la Cruz, B. Flores, and E. Garcia. 1986. Beginning literacy development, learning, and evolution across social contexts: Collaborative action research. Paper presented at the NABE 15th Annual International Bilingual/Bicultural Education Conference, Chicago.

Collier, V. P. 1995a. Acquiring a second language for school. *Directions in Language & Education,* 1(4).Washington, DC: National Clearinghouse for Bilingual Education.

Collier, V. P. 1995b. *Promoting academic success for ESL students: Understanding second language acquisition for school.* Elizabeth, NJ: New Jersey Teachers of English to Speakers of Other Languages-Bilingual Education.

Collins, M. and C. Tamarkin. 1990. *Marva Collins' way.* Los Angeles: Jeremy P. Tarcher.

Cummins, J. 1980. The entry and exit fallacy in bilingual education. *NABE Journal* 4(2): 25-59.

Cummins, J. 1984. *Bilingualism and special education: Issues in assessment and pedagogy.* San Diego: College-Hill Press.

Cummins, J. 1986. Empowering minority students: A framework for intervention. *Harvard Education Review* 56: 18-36.

Cummins, J. 1989. *Empowering minority students.* Sacramento, CA: California Association for Bilingual Education.

Cummins, J., and D. Sayers. 1995. *Brave new schools: Challenging cultural illiteracy through global learning networks.* New York: St. Martin's Press.

Davison, D., and J. Reyner. 1992. American Indian bilingual education: "Whole mathematics." *NABE News* 16(2): 4-5.

DeVillar, R. A., and C. J. Faltis. 1991. *Computers and cultural diversity: Restructuring for school success.* Albany, NY: State University of New York Press.

Doris, E. 1991. *Doing what scientists do: Children learn to investigate their world.* Portsmouth, NH: Heinemann.

Edelsky, C. 1986. *Writing in a bilingual program: Había una vez.* Norwood, NJ: Ablex.

Edelsky, C. 1991. *With literacy and justice for all: Rethinking the social in language and education.* London: The Falmer Press.

Edelsky, C., B. Altwerger, and B. Flores. 1991. *Whole language: What's the difference?* Portsmouth, NH: Heinemann.

Edelsky, C., with S. Harman. 1991. One more critique of testing—with two differences. In *With literacy and justice for all: Rethinking the social in language and education,* by C. Edelsky. London: The Falmer Press.

Enright, D. S., and M. L. McCloskey. 1988. *Integrating English: Developing English language and literacy in the multilingual classroom.* Reading, MA: Addison-Wesley.

Escamilla, K. 1994. The sociolinguistic environment of a bilingual school: A case study introduction. *Bilingual Research Journal* 18: 21-47.

Faltis, C. 1990. New directions in bilingual research design: The study of interactive decision making. In *Language distribution issues in bilingual schooling,* edited by R. Jacobson and C. Faltis. Clevedon, England: Multilingual Matters

Faltis, C. J., and R. A. DeVillar, eds. 1990. Language minority students and computers [Special issue]. *Computers in the Schools* 7(1/2)

Frankenstein, M. 1987. Critical mathematics education: An application of Paulo Freire's epistemology. In *Freire for the classroom: A sourcebook for liberatory teaching,* edited by I. Shor. Portsmouth, NH: Heinemann Boynton/Cook Publishers.

Freeman, D. E., and Y. S. Freeman. 1991. "Doing" social studies: Whole language lessons to promote social action. *Social education* (January): 29-32, 66.

Freeman, Y. S. , and D. E. Freeman. 1997. *Teaching reading and writing in Spanish in the bilingual classroom.* Portsmouth, NH: Heinemann.

Freire, P. 1970. *Pedagogy of the oppressed.* New York: Continuum.

Freire, P. 1973. *Education for critical consciousness.* New York: Seabury.

Garcia, E., E. H. Garcia, K. Kaczmarek, G. Hidalgo, G. Gonzalez, and B. Flores. 1989. Effective schooling for Hispanic linguistic minority students. Symposium presented at the NABE 18th Annual International Bilingual/Bicultural Education Conference, Miami.

González-Edfelt, N. 1990. Oral interaction and collaboration at the computer:

Learning English as a second language with the help of your peers. *Computers in the Schools* 7(1/2): 53-90.

Grosjean, F. 1982. *Life with two languages: An introduction to bilingualism.* Cambridge, MA: Harvard University Press.

Heath, S. B. 1983. Learners as ethnographers. In *Ways with words: Language, life and work in communities and classrooms.* Cambridge, UK: Cambridge University Press.

Heath, S. B. 1985. Literacy or literate skills? Considerations for ESL/EFL learners. In *On TESOL '84: A brave new world for TESOL,* edited by P. Larson, E. L. Judd, and D. S. Messerschmitt. Washington, DC: Teachers of English to Speakers of Other Languages.

Holdaway, D. 1979. *Foundations of literacy.* Sydney: Ashton Scholastic.

Hudelson, S. 1989. "Teaching" English through content-area activities. In *When they don't all speak English: Integrating the ESL student into the regular classroom,* edited by P. Rigg and V. G. Allen. Urbana, IL: National Council of Teachers of English.

Huerta-Macías, A., and E. Quintero. 1992. Code-switching, bilingualism, and biliteracy: A case study. *Bilingual Research Journal* 16: 69-90.

Jacobson, R. 1981. The implementation of a bilingual instructional model: The New Concurrent Approach. In *Ethnoperspectives in bilingual education research, Vol. 3: Bilingual education technology,* edited by R. V. Padilla. Ypsilanti, MI: Eastern Michigan University.

Jacobson, R. 1990. Allocating two languages as a key feature of a bilingual methodology. In *Language Distribution Issues in Bilingual Schooling,* edited by R. Jacobson and C. Faltis Clevedon, England: Multilingual Matters Ltd.

Jacobson, R., and C. Faltis, eds. 1990. *Language distribution issues in bilingual schooling.* Clevedon, England: Multilingual Matters Ltd.

Jones, T. G. 1993. Biliteracy from the student's point of view. In *The power of two languages: Literacy and biliteracy for Spanish-speaking students,* edited by J. V. Tinajero and A. F. Ada. New York and Columbus: Macmillan/McGraw-Hill School Publishing.

Jordan, C. 1995. Creating cultures of schooling: Historical and conceptual background of the KEEP/Rough Rock collaboration. *Bilingual Research Journal* 19: 83-100.

Lessow-Hurley, J. 1996. *Foundations of dual language instruction,* 2nd ed. White Plains, NY: Longman.

Legarreta, D. 1977. Language choice in bilingual classrooms. *TESOL Quarterly* 11: 9-16.

Levy, S. 1996. *Starting from scratch: One classroom builds its own curriculum.* Portsmouth, NH: Heinemann.

MacGowan, A. 1986. Interactions and transactions during literacy activities in a bilingual first grade: An ethnographic study. Ed.D. dissertation, Boston University.

McCollum, P. 1994. Language use in two-way bilingual programs. *IDRA Newsletter* 21(2): 1, 9-11.

Milk, R. D. 1990. Integrating language and content: Implications for language distribution in bilingual classrooms. In *Language distribution issues in bilingual schooling,* edited by R. Jacobson and C. Faltis. Clevedon, England: Multilingual Matters Ltd.

Navarrete, C., J. Wilde, C. Nelson, R. Martínez, and G. Hargett. 1990. *Informal assessment in educational evaluation: Implications for bilingual education programs.* Program Information Guide Series No. 3. Washington, DC: National Clearinghouse for Bilingual Education.

Ovando, C. J., and V. Collier. 1985. Culture. In *Bilingual and ESL Classrooms: Teaching in multicultural contexts*. New York: McGraw-Hill.

Pease-Alvarez, L., and O. A. Vásquez. 1990. Sharing language and technical expertise around the computer. In *Computers in the Schools* 7(1/2): 91-107.

Pennycook, A. 1989. The concept of method, interested knowledge, and the politics of language teaching. *TESOL Quarterly* 23: 589-618.

Pérez, B., and M. E. Torres-Guzmán. 1996. *Learning in two worlds: An integrated Spanish/English biliteracy approach,* 2d ed. White Plains, NY: Longman.

Peterson, R. E. 1991. Teaching how to read the world and change it: Critical pedagogy in the intermediate grades. In *Literacy as praxis: Culture, language, and pedagogy*, edited by C. E. Walsh. Norwood, NJ: Ablex.

Peyton, J. K., and T. Batson. 1986. Computer networking: Making connections between speech and writing. *ERIC/CLL News Bulletin* 10(1): 1, 5-7.

Pierce, L. V., and J. M. O'Malley. 1992. *Performance and portfolio assessment for language minority students.* Program Information Guide Series No. 9. Washington, DC: National Clearinghouse for Bilingual Education.

Poplin, M. S. 1993. Making our whole language bilingual classrooms also liberatory. In *The power of two languages: Literacy and biliteracy for Spanish-speaking students*, edited by J. V. Tinajero and A. F. Ada. New York: Macmillan/McGraw-Hill School Publishing.

Prabhu, N. S. 1990. There is no best method—why? *TESOL Quarterly* 24; 161-176.

Richards, J. C., and T. Rodgers. 1982. Method: Approach, design and procedure. *TESOL Quarterly* 16: 153-168.

Romero, M., and A. Parrino. 1994. Planned Alternation of Languages (PAL): Language use and distribution in bilingual classrooms. *The Journal of Educational Issues of Linguistic Minority Students* 13: 132-161.

Romero, T., G. Hidalgo, K. Kaczmarek, E. Garcia, and B. Flores. 1987. Thematic units—A way to provide meaningful curriculum for all students in your class, using their interests, their language. Workshop presented at the NABE 17th Annual International Bilingual/Bicultural Education Conference, Denver.

Rose, M. 1995. *Possible lives: The promise of public education in America.* Boston: Houghton Mifflin.

Rosebery, A.S., B. Warren, and F. R. Conant. 1992. *Appropriating scientific discourse: Findings from language minority classrooms.* Santa Cruz, CA: The National Center for Research on Cultural Diversity and Second Language Learning.

Rowan, T. E., and B. Bourne. 1994. *Thinking like mathematicians: Putting the K-4 NCTM standards into practice.* Portsmouth, NH: Heinemann.

Saville, M. R., and R. C. Troike. 1971. *A handbook of bilingual education,* rev. ed. Washington, DC: TESOL.

Sayers, D. 1986. Sending messages across the classroom and around the world. *TESOL Newsletter* 20 (suppl. 3): 7-8.

Sayers, D. 1993. Helping students find their voice in nonfiction writing: Team-teaching partnerships between distant classes. In *The power of two languages: Literacy and biliteracy for Spanish-speaking students*, edited by J. V. Tinajero and A. F. Ada. New York: Macmillan/McGraw-Hill School Publishing.

Sayers, D., and K. Brown. 1987. Bilingual education and telecommunications: A perfect fit. *The Computing Teacher* 17: 23-24.

Shor, I. 1987. *Freire for the classroom: A sourcebook for liberatory teaching.* Portsmouth, NH: Heinemann Boynton/Cook Publishers.

Smith, D., P. Gilmore, S. Goldman, and R. McDermott. 1993. Failure's failure. In *Minority education: Anthropological perspectives*, edited by E. Jacob and C. Jordan. Norwood, NJ: Ablex.

Smith, F. 1975. *Comprehension and learning: A conceptual framework for teachers.* New York: Holt, Rinehart & Winston.

Smith, F. 1986. *Insult to intelligence: The bureaucratic invasion of our classrooms.* Portsmouth, NH: Heinemann.

Tikunoff, W. J., and J. A. Vázquez-Faria. 1982. Successful instruction for bilingual schooling. *Peabody Journal of Education* 59: 234-271.

Trueba, H. T. 1989. *Raising silent voices: Educating the linguistic minorities for the 21st century.* Cambridge, MA: Newbury House Publishers.

Ulibarri, D. M., M. L. Spencer, and G. A. Rivas. 1981. Language proficiency and academic achievement: A study of language proficiency tests and their relationship to school ratings as predictors of academic achievement. *NABE Journal 5:* 47-80.

Valdés, G., and R. A. Figueroa. 1994. *Bilingualism and testing: A special case of bias.* Norwood, NJ: Ablex.

Wallerstein, N. 1987. Problem-posing education: Freire's method for transformation. In *Freire for the classroom: A sourcebook for liberatory teaching*, edited by I. Shor. Portsmouth, NH: Heinemann.

Walsh, C. E., (ed.). 1991. *Literacy as praxis: Culture, language, and pedagogy.* Norwood, NJ: Ablex.

Walsh, C. E. 1993. Becoming critical: Rethinking literacy, language, and teaching. In *The power of two languages: Literacy and biliteracy for Spanish-speaking students*, edited by J. V. Tinajero and A. F. Ada. New York: Macmillan/McGraw-Hill School Publishing.

Wells, G., and G. L. Chang-Wells. 1992. *Constructing knowledge together: Classrooms as centers of inquiry and literacy.* Portsmouth, NH: Heinemann.

White, C. 1990. *Jevon doesn't sit at the back anymore.* Teachers' Forum Series. Toronto: Scholastic.

Whitmore, K. F., and C. G. Crowell. 1994. *Inventing a classroom: Life in a bilingual, whole language learning community.* York, ME: Stenhouse Publishers.

Woodward, H. 1994. *Negotiated evaluation: Involving children and parents in the process.* Portsmouth, NH: Heinemann.

Wong Fillmore, L. 1982. Instructional language as linguistic input: Second language learning in classrooms. In *Communicating in the classroom*, edited by L. C. Wilkinson. New York: Academic Press.

Young, K. A. 1994. *Constructing buildings, bridges, and minds: Building an integrated curriculum through social studies.* Portsmouth, NH: Heinemann.